Collecting American Brilliant Cut Glass

1876-1916

Bill and Louise Boggess

Schiffer Publishing Ltd

1469 Morstein Road, West Chester, Pennsylvania 19380

Dedicated to our children

Patricia Anne and Howard Blair
Constance and William F. Boggess III

ALSO BY LOUISE BOGGESS:

FICTION TECHNIQUES THAT SELL
WRITING ARTICLES THAT SELL
WRITING FILLERS THAT SELL
JOURNEY TO CITIZENSHIP
YOUR SOCIAL SECURITY BENEFITS
ARTICLE TECHNIQUES THAT SELL
WRITING FICTION THAT SELLS
HOW TO WRITE FILLERS AND SHORT
    FEATURES THAT SELL
HOW TO WRITE SHORT STORIES THAT
    SELL

Audio Cassettes
HOW TO WRITE SHORT STORIES THAT
    SELL
ARTICLE TECHNIQUES THAT SELL

Video Cassettes
HOW TO WRITE SHORT STORIES THAT
    SELL
ARTICLE TECHNIQUES THAT SELL

WITH HUSBAND BILL:
AMERICAN BRILLIANT CUT GLASS
IDENTIFYING AMERICAN BRILLIANT CUT
    GLASS
IDENTIFYING AMERICAN BRILLIANT CUT
    GLASS Revised and Enlarged Edition

Key for Price Guide
S = Standard cut   C = Choice, has extra features
P = Premium   L = Limited

To simplify and make the Value Guide more usable, we have divided all illustrations into four categories: Standard, Choice, Premium, and Limited.

A STANDARD piece consists of a clear blank, fairly simple pattern, and a common shape.

A CHOICE piece adds these features to the standard characteristics: more ornate pattern, larger or smaller size, variance in shape, and a quality addition of a lid, handles, or foot.

A PREMIUM piece retains the best features of a Standard and Choice one and combines them with sharpness in cutting, very ornate or highly simplified pattern, excellent polish, unique shape, and at least one or more quality extras.

LIMITED describes museum-type pieces that defy evaluation but depend on what the buyer will pay.

Before each caption number of an illustration, we have placed the key letter of the classification: S, C, P, and L. To effectively use the Value Guide, find an illustration comparable to your piece in shape and pattern. It need not exactly duplicate your piece. Find the shape and the letter in the Value Guide to learn the price range.

Published by Schiffer Publishing, Ltd.
1469 Morstein Road
West Chester, Pennsylvania 19380
Please write for a free catalog.
This book may be purchased from the publisher.
Please include $2.00 postage.
Try your bookstore first.

Contents

Acknowledgments

This book represents the combined effort of so many who share our appreciation of American brilliant cut glass.

We greatly appreciate the special research and pictures from the following: Walter Poeth, Jane and Max Redden, Isabelle Middleton, Martin Folb, Walter Germer, Robert Peavy, and Jean Wright. James D. McMahon and Carol Buskirk of the Hershey Museum supplied information on the Hershey lamp, and Rene Lawrie of the Lightner Museum sent pictures that included the Hawkes floor lamp.

Several collectors let us photograph their highly prized, one-of-a-kind pieces: Bob and Garnett Hall, Bill and Dola Beckman, Ed and Janet Beach, and Ralph Girkins. Dowlton and Anne Berry sent colored slides when we needed them. So many contributed photographs of unusual shapes. Bob Loomis and Hal Barnes rescued us when we needed some special sketches.

We particularly express our gratitude to Peter and Nancy Schiffer, our editors, who extended the deadline on the book and suggested a new plan for submitting the manuscript. Finally, a very genuine thanks goes to Sam and Becky Story and those listed below because they believed in us and encouraged us to write this book: Irma Adams, Harry and Irene Aubright, Ian and Maggie Berke, Carol Birt, Howard and Pat Blair, Lila Bloomfield, Mike Brookshire, Bustamente Enterprises, Lynda Carregan, Albin and Frances Chalk, Barbara Chamberlin, Abe Chartman, George Clark, Glen and Dolores Clause, Price Corny, Patrick Curry, Bob and Shirley Des Lauriers, George Dittmar, Barbara Doble, Paul and Pam Donath, Mrs. Duncan W. Dougherty, Ann Dunlap, George Durnford, Ray and Sharon Eliggi, Harry and Rosemary Estes, Walter Frome, John and Joan Glenn, Dr. Jon Hall, Bob and Jerry Hampton, Dorothy Harrington, Jim Haven, R. F. Hawkins, Bob and Betty Haynes, Marie Hegarity, Betty Houston, Claire Hohsteim, Alfred Huddleston, Dr. and Mrs. Hunt, George Hunt, William Jarvis, Joyce Jenson, Janet Jerome, Paul and Midge Keller, Frank and Randi Kelly, J. Kimberling, Keith Kinkade, Dave and Rita Klyce, George Kovatch, Dean and Sally Jo Kregger, Bob and Doris LaSalle, Gil and Gloria Lopez, Eleanor Lovett, Madeline Lundin, Carrol Lyle, Howard McFarland, Tom Matthews, Marion Mickaels, Carol Miller, Larry Milot, Wayne Montano, C. W. Moody, Garth Mowery, Dorothy Murphy, Eugene Murray, Conrad and Ellie Nelson, Ivadell Nordheim, Tom and Theresa O'Connell, Alice Otten, Doris Patterson, Mary Patterson, Mrs. Jack Pelzner, Alice Peri, Roscoe Penrod, Thelma Prouse, Richard and Joan Randles, Dorothy Reynolds, Jean Reith, Kevin Ross, Harold Rothberg, Robert and Barbara Scott, Catheryn Sears, Shull's Piano Antiques, Marilyn Simpson, Ardene Fairchild Smith, Trula Smith, Sharalyn Spiteri, Kim Strutt, S. Lee Teed, Del and Elone Tipps, Alexander and Lorene Tisnado, Bob Toby, Tresham Collection, Virginia Tubb, Mr. and Mrs. Jack Walker, Richard Wean, Dallas Wertzberger, Ron and Marilyn Wessen, Bob and Carol Weir, Phil and Katharyn Yonge, Dorothy Zink

*P*reface

Beauty intoxicates both the holder and beholder...
James Thomson

This book presents a logical, step-by-step approach to collecting American brilliant cut glass. You start with the pieces you already own and then expand your knowledge in buying, locating signatures, identifying patterns, and recognizing plus values. The book concludes with suggestions for maintaining a collection. Anyone can easily follow these directions and become a collector.

From our first book, AMERICAN BRILLIANT CUT GLASS—now out of print—we have updated applicable sections and identified 192 patterns by catalog name from it. Those patterns already identified we did not repeat except for a very few comparisons. When we did repeat a pattern, we pictured a different shape.

We have added a large number of new identifications from 126 catalogs, magazine advertising, and patent records. For a simplified value guide we have divided all patterns into three categories: standard, choice, and premium and provided a price range. Some pieces no one can evaluate, so we have marked them "limited." We have received special information from collectors and dealers that has helped us authenticate new facts.

You will find two sections of special interest: we picture and discuss historical pieces and some very outstanding ones to dream of owning some day. The book contains 1068 photographs of glass owned by collectors. In referring to factories or cutting shops, we have stated the full name of the company when first mentioned. From then on we use a shortened name, such as Libbey or Hawkes.

We have earnestly tried to accurately match photographs of cut glass in every detail to illustrations in catalogs or other sources. If we have erred—and we could very easily—we honestly tried.

By no means do we consider research on cut glass complete. Tomorrow will bring more information. One fact remains the same: the United States produced the finest cut glass in the world. Never forget it!

P 1. A 9-inch bowl cut in an ornate pattern with hobstars.

Chapter 1
The Starting Point

C 2. A 5-inch nappy with a single, decorated handle.

S 3. A 7-inch nappy with two handles.

S 4. A 6-inch nappy with triple handles.

At an antiques show a woman stared longingly at a beautiful, cut glass bowl featured in a dealer's display. "Do you collect cut glass?" the dealer asked.

"Not really, but I love it. Now and then I buy a piece I can afford. I guess you'd call me an accumulator rather than a collector," she added with a laugh.

If you have accumulated some pieces of cut glass, why not become a collector? As a collector you not only consider the price but learn facts about cut glass that make you a more informed buyer. So start your collecting by learning about the pieces you already own.

SEEK KNOWLEDGE

Knowledge and collecting go together. Fortunately, you can acquire much of this information through the following sources at your library.

1. Reference Books

At most public libraries you can check out books on American brilliant cut glass—even those out of print.

From the bibliography of this book make a list of references. If your library does not have copies of them, usually the research librarian can secure them on library loan. First read those that give general information on cut glass.

General References: These books normally contain a brief history of the Brilliant Period (1876-1916) and provide information on the production process. Such information includes making the molten glass (metal), blowing the blank (shape), and steps in cutting the pattern.

Most explain that two types of companies produced cut glass: a factory and a cutting shop. A factory made the metal, blew the blank, created and cut the pattern—the entire process. The cutting shop bought the blank from the factory, designed the pattern, and cut the blank. Both types of companies sold to wholesalers, shops or stores, and individuals.

Specific Companies: A number of reference books focus on one particular company, such as:

C. Dorflinger & Sons	Libbey Glass Company
H. C. Fry Glass Company	Pairpoint Glass Company
T. G. Hawkes & Company	H. P. Sinclaire & Company

Most of these contain reprints of old catalogs for pattern identification.

Collecting Information: Several books emphasize identification of patterns. When unable to identify a pattern by company name, certain books do improvise a descriptive one. Always look for an identification by catalog name.

2. Magazine Articles

Current antiques magazines frequently supplement books with recent research. Your library subscribes to several of these magazines that periodically publish articles on cut glass. Most libraries make back issues available.

3. American Cut Glass Association

Membership in the American Cut Glass Association will guide you in becoming a more informed collector. This national organization publishes a monthly newsletter that includes useful information—old and new—on cut glass. One program of the Association reprints old cut glass catalogs for sale and another aids in matching pieces to complete a set. To contact the Association write K. Emmerson, P.O. Box 482, Ramona, CA. 92065

At the Association's annual convention held in various cities across the United States, you meet dealers and collectors, hear knowledgeable speakers, and gather new information. In different areas of the United States, regional chapters have organized and meet regularly. No doubt, you can find such a chapter in your vicinity or through the national Association. Through this organization and dealers you can make friends with other collectors.

4. Cut Glass Dealers

Dealers who specialize in selling cut glass have accumulated a great deal of knowledge. Many will share their knowledge learned from research, contact with knowledgeable collectors, and their own experiences in buying and selling.

Knowledge pays excellent dividends. You soon realize that the more you learn, the more you want to know. Most important, your knowledge provides you with the confidence to collect. As you read the text, study the illustrations at the same time. This procedure will focus the information for you.

PLAN A COLLECTION

We asked groups of dealers and experienced collectors to recommend pieces for a beginning collection. From these interviews, we have compiled a list that takes into consideration lower prices, plentiful supply, and useful pieces for entertaining. Since some companies differ slightly as to the name of a shape, we have selected the terms most commonly used in the catalogs.

1. Nappy

The term "nappy" comes from old English "napier" and refers to a small bowl. The round nappy in cut glass measures five to seven inches in diameter and approximately an inch in depth. Your choices include those with one handle (C 2), two (S 3), three (S 4), or none (S 5). A few companies added peg feet to those with no handles (S 6). Do not confuse the five-inch nappy with the four and one-half inch saucer that formed a set with the berry bowl.

S 5. A 5-inch nappy with no handles, but signed Clark in the Victor Pattern.

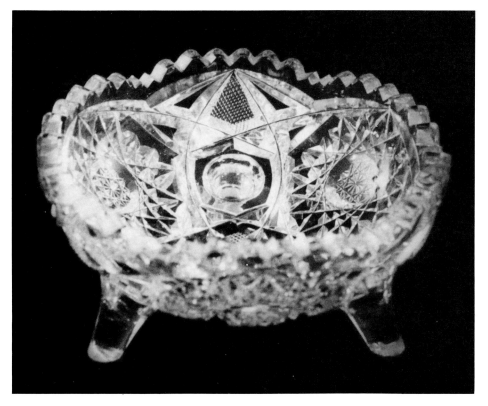

S 6. A 6-inch nappy with peg feet and no handles.

S 7. A 4.5-inch saucer in Sunburst Pattern by Unger.

S 8. An 8-inch bowl in Sunburst Pattern by Unger that matches the saucer.

S 9. A 4.5-inch saucer with a round handle.

2. Bowls and Saucers

Companies produced an abundance of bowls with varying dimensions. The berry bowl measured, seven, eight, nine, and ten inches in diameter and three and one-half in depth. Companies cut small saucers (S 7) of one inch in depth and four and one-half inches in diameter to match the berry bowl (S 8). For an extra fee, the company would add a round handle (S 9). Do not mistake this saucer for a nappy.

Rarely will you find a bowl and matching saucers in a set. Buy the bowl and shop for the matching saucers to make a set. The patterns on these bowls range from simple (S 10) to ornate (C 11). Several catalogs call the small, seven-inch bowl "whipped cream" (S 12), a real "find."

Because of the popularity of bowls, companies produced other types with specific identification. Low bowls came in the same dimensions as the berry ones but with a depth of two and one-half inches (S 13). Fruit inspired other shapes in bowls. The orange bowl retained the depth of the berry one but had an oval shape with rounded ends. It varied in length from seven to ten inches (C 14). The fruit bowl also has an oval shape but with more pointed ends (C 15).

If you don't already own a punch bowl, wait until you learn more about cut glass. The diameters of punch bowls measure twelve, fourteen, and sixteen inches. Generally speaking, the height almost equals the diameter. Companies produced them as a single bowl (P 16) or as a bowl and foot (P 17).

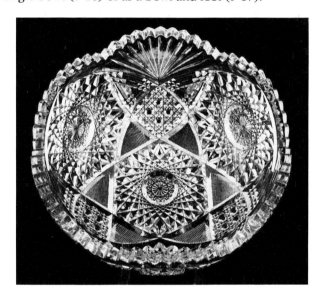

S 10. A simple pattern in a 10-bowl.

C 11. A 9-inch bowl in an ornate pattern.

S 12. A 7-inch whipped cream bowl signed Clark.

S 13. An 8-inch low bowl.

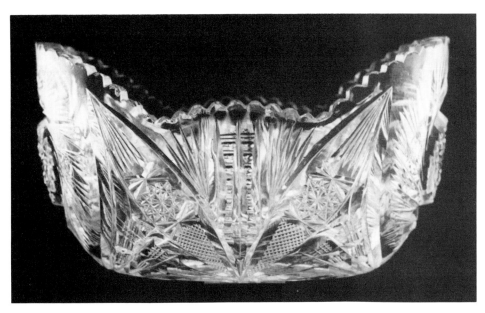

S 14. An orange bowl measuring 8 by 4 inches.

C 15. A fruit bowl that measures 14 by 8.25
inches.

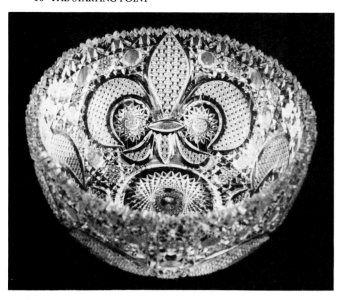

P 16. A 12-inch punch bowl.

P 17. A two-piece punch bowl in the same pattern that measures 18 inches in diameter and 12 inches in height.

3. Celery

Oval celeries measure eleven to thirteen inches in length, approximately four in width, and two in depth. Most collections contain two or more celeries because of the beauty and usefulness (S 18). The more desirable ones have a scalloped, saw-tooth rim and turned over edge (C 19).

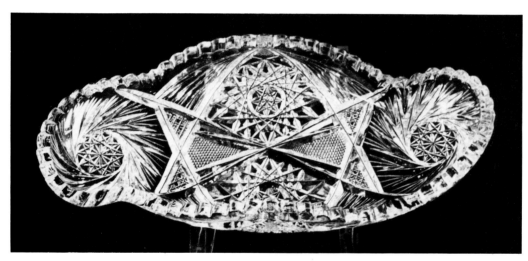

S 18. An 11-inch celery in S-shape will add to any basic collection.

S 19. A 12-inch celery with turned over sides.

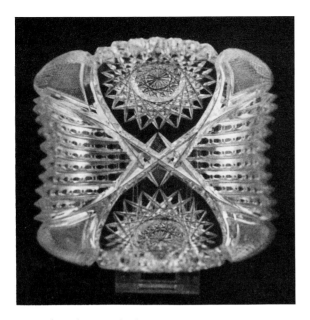

S 20. A 4.5-inch, square bonbon.

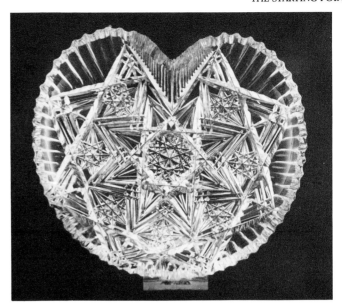

S 21. A 7-inch, heart bonbon in Salem Pattern by Pairpoint Corporation.

4. Bonbon

All companies cut small, shallow pieces called bonbons in a variety of shapes: square (S 20), heart (S 21), and triangular (S 22), to name the most popular. A triangular bonbon occasionally applied a handle on one side (C 23), and a round one added a stick-like handle to the center (C 24). Sometimes the craftsman cut a thumbhold similar to a spout at one end (C 25). Possibly you already own a bonbon or plan to add one or two to your collection.

S 22. A 5.5-inch, triangular bonbon.

C 23. An 8 by 4 inch, triangular bonbon with a handle in Royal Pattern by Hunt Glass Company.

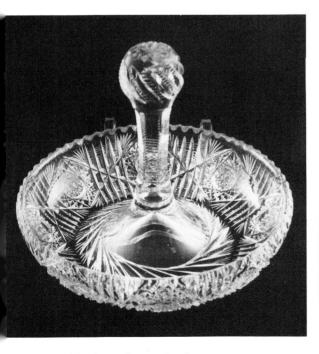

C 24. A 9.5-inch bonbon with center handle in Bedford Pattern by J. D. Bergen Company.

C 25. A 7-inch bonbon with a spout handle in Sultana Pattern by Blackmer Cut Glass Company.

C 26. A 7-inch tall carafe with hobstar dominance.

5. Carafe

A carafe adds variety to a collection, sells at a medium price, and functions for serving drinks. The piece consists of a long curved neck that joined a ball-like base. The ball part included such shapes as: squat (C 26), tapering (C 27), or round (C 28). An eye opener, a special type of carafe, also contained a tumbler that fit over the neck (C 29). Look at a number of carafes before you buy.

C 27. An 8.5-inch tall carafe in Coral Pattern by Quaker City Glass Company.

C 28. A 7-inch tall carafe in Pattern #9130 and signed Hoare by J. Hoare & Company.

C 29. A 7-inch, eye-opener carafe in Strawberry Diamond Pattern.

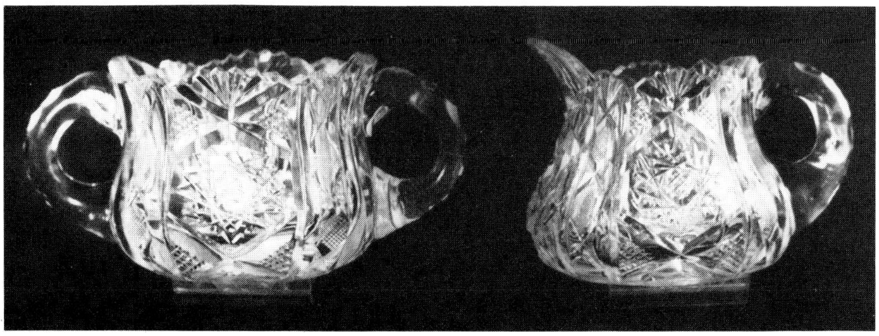

S 30. A small sugar and cream.

6. Sugar and Cream

Every collector needs a sugar and cream set because you can use it frequently. While you find them in small (S 30), medium (S 31), and large (C 32), most collectors tend to buy the middle size. Most likely, you already own a set.

S 31. A medium sized sugar and cream with base.

C 32. A large sugar and cream on a foot.

S 33. A 7-inch relish.

7. Pickle or Relish

Catalogs list these small pieces as pickle or relish. Oval in shape, they measure si[...]
to seven inches in length and three to four in width (S 33). A slight twist in one (C
34) or a smaller shape (S 35) makes them more desirable. The different uses for th[...]
relish and the abundance of the supply makes collecting them easy. When you buy[...]
focus on interesting patterns and unusual shapes.

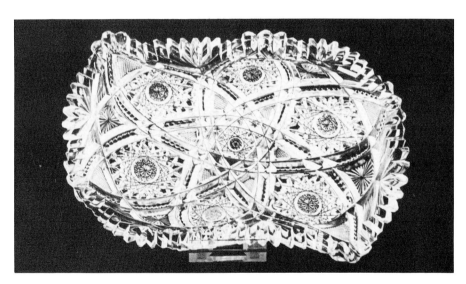

C 34. A 7.5 by 4 inches relish in s-shape.

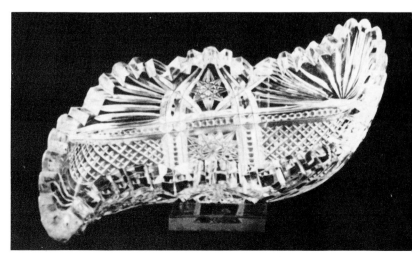

S 35. A 7-inch relish in a narrow s-shape.

8. Vase

No piece of cut glass rivals the vase in choices of shapes, such as: cylindral (C 36), footed (S 37), curved (C 38), or urn type (C 39)—the list goes on endlessly. Not only does the vase come in varied shapes but also in all sizes from a height of three to twenty inches or more. Always consider what you like and where you plan to use the vase when you buy one or more for your collection.

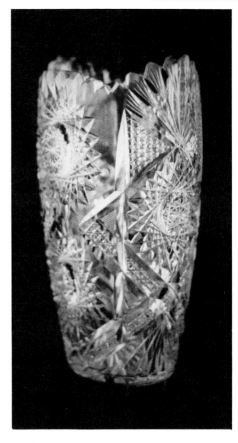

C 36. A round vase, 9 inches tall and 6 inches in diameter.

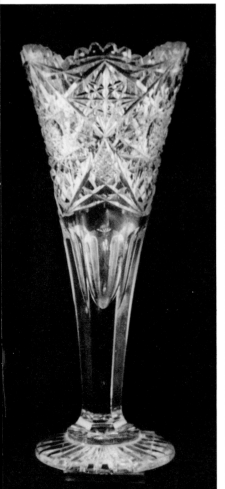

37. An 8-inch tall vase in a popular shape with foot.

C 38. A vase, 14 inches tall and 6 inches in diameter, with a bulbous shape.

C 39. A thirteen-inch vase with an urn shape.

S 40. A salt and pepper set, 3.5 inches tall.

S 41. Footed toothpick holder, 3.5-inches tall.

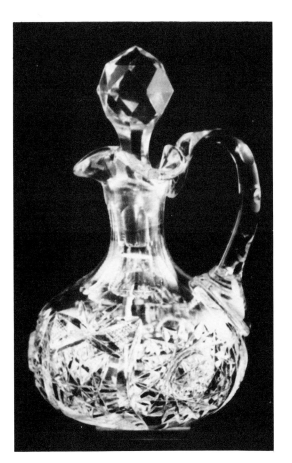

S 42. A 5-inch tall oil.

9. Small Pieces

Most collections contain interesting small pieces, some of which you may use every day, such as a salt and pepper shaker (S 40). A toothpick holder easily becomes a conversational piece (S 41). An oil—not cruet, a later term—adds grace to a dinner table (S 42). As you shop for the larger pieces, do look for butter pats (S 43), individual salts (S 44) or any other inexpensive, small piece.

Compare this list for a beginning collection with the pieces you already own and decide on probable additions. In fact, you may start a most-wanted list to take with you when you shop for cut glass.

SHOPPING SPOTS

Observation offers one key to effective buying, so apply your knowledge at every opportunity. The more pieces you see, the more opportunity to become an informed buyer. Most collectors soon learn where to buy cut glass and check these spots regularly. Some of these you already know, and others you will discover for yourself.

1. Antique Shows

At a show you meet two types of dealers: the specialist who handles mostly cut glass and the general who displays only a few pieces. The large dealers who occupy the choice locations at a show and sell cut glass exclusively prove most knowledgeable and offer quality pieces for sale.

When you find a piece you like, ask the dealer for any information regarding it. By all means, volunteer your interest in buying the piece. Ask the dealer for the best price when you purchase an expensive item or several pieces. Most dealers price to reduce a certain amount. Sometimes the dealer volunteers a discount or suggests a reduced price. Never make an offer!

2. Shops and Collectives

After a show, follow up your contact with the dealers located in your area and ask their help in finding pieces on your "want" list. Recently dealers have joined together and rented a large building where each occupied a space for display. These collectives, unlike a show, provide daily contact with a number of dealers. Check the yellow pages of your telephone directory under "antiques" for the locations of collectives near you.

Use the yellow pages to find shops when visiting briefly in an unfamiliar town. Some of them will list cut glass in the advertisement. When you telephone a shop and inquire about cut glass, the person often provides the names of such dealers. Occasionally, antiques dealer associations in a town or city supplies you with a local map that lists antiques shops. The National Association of Dealers in Antiques, Inc. publishes one, as do various state organizations and antiques magazines. A few shops sell small booklets listing dealers in specific areas, such as Western United States.

3. House or Estate Sales

Sometimes the heirs of an estate will hold a sale directly on the property or hire a person who makes a business of liquidating estates. Watch the classified advertisements for antiques in the local or nearby newspapers for announcements.

4. Flea Markets

Flea markets consist of two types: permanent ones open regularly on weekends or sporadic ones sponsored by clubs, churches, or civic organizations as a fund raiser. The second type offers more bargains. At a regular flea markets, shop with the "one-timers" or the "ground spreaders." These sellers include people moving into a smaller home and need to get rid of some possessions, heirs who have no use for what they inherited, or collectors upgrading a collection.

5. Garage or Rummage Sales

These sales offer a one or two day mini-flea market. Sometimes several individuals get together and do a garage sale. Churches or civic organizations call for donations from members for such a sale. A few churches have a permanent room to house any donations by members during the year.

6. Auctions

Frequently auction houses concentrate on an all-cut-glass sale. Your research librarian can provide you with addresses of major auction houses, so write them for a catalog of upcoming sales. The collector who cannot attend an auction may preview the catalog or the auction and make a written bid for a small fee.

7. Unclaimed Storage

A few warehouses have a show room where they display unclaimed storage. When the storage bill exceeds the value, the company sells the items to pay the bill.

8. Advertisements

Antiques magazines and newspapers run advertisements to sell cut glass. Anyone who buys glass by this method needs to have a clear understanding as to the condition of the piece and the sale terms.

9. Individual Initiative

Collectors with imagination and initiative have found quality cut glass. When one collector plans her itinerary for a vacation, she advertises for cut glass in the local newspaper a day or two before she arrives.

By all means let others know that you collect cut glass. Word of mouth works wonders. So put your imagination to work and initiate some new locations for cut glass treasures. Collecting cut glass not only involves what to buy and where to find it but how to buy.

S 43. A square, 2.5-inch butter pat.

S 44. An individual salt, #800 signed Hawkes.

Chapter 2
Guidelines for Buying

S 45. A 5-inch finger bowl with a chip on the rim a repair can remove.

DAMAGED GLASS

Knowledge and experience rank as the best teachers in buying cut glass. Yet you need not rely entirely on your present knowledge or personal experiences. A number of collectors and dealers have made mistakes, such as failing to spot defects that reduce the value of cut glass. We have made our share, but forewarned means forearmed.

We interviewed a group of collectors and dealers on what to check and how to avoid errors in buying. From these interviews we compiled some guidelines to help you avoid mistakes in buying.

Cut glass proves quite fragile because of prior usage and age. Most dealers list cut glass as "mint" meaning perfect condition; slight defects, such as those not readily seen; or "as is" to indicate obvious damage. Since cut glass came off the production line seventy to one hundred years ago, few pieces remain completely undamaged today.

Occasionally you find the exception, a piece tucked away in a cabinet and never used for fear of breaking. Therefore, follow the dictate of serious collectors and careful dealers by taking along a pocket magnifying glass to detect difficult-to-see defects when you shop for cut glass.

P 46. A 16-inch, tubular vase with rims that can chip easily.

P 47. A 12-inch decanter that may chip on the rim or neck ring.

C 48. A 10-inch bowl with a mint, scolloped rim.

1. Chips

A chip refers to a nick broken from a rim or a miter on a piece of cut glass (S 45). Age, heavy cutting, and careless handling causes certain pieces of cut glass to chip more than others. Chips appear principally along the top edge of a vase (P 46), a decanter (P 47), bowls (C 48), comport (S 49), or jug (C 50). Old catalogs use the term "comport" rather than "compote" and "jug" rather than "pitcher." At times an entire tooth may get knocked off a serrated edge.

S 49. Careful usage will keep the rim of this 10-inch tall comport in mint condition.

C 50. The rim or base of this 12-inch jug can chip easily with careless handling.

P 51. The sawtooth rim and scolloped foot of this 11-inch cake tray will stay mint with careful usage.

S 52. Tumblers chip easily on the rim and base because of usage.

Slight nicks do occur on deeply cut miters when pieces bump against the wall of a cabinet or against each other during an earthquake or a cyclone. Examine the edge of a footed piece, as a cake tray (P 51), the base of a tumbler (S 52), or on the rim of a covered cheese and plate (C 53) for chips. Educate your fingers through practice to feel any chip, no matter how slight. Most sellers expect this scrutiny from prospective buyers, especially of expensive pieces.

C 53. The 8-inch tall dome of a cheese in Brunswick from Higgins & Seiter requires care when replacing it on the plate to prevent chipping.

S 54. This heavy, 12-inch tray needs careful handling to avoid flaking on the deep miters.

S 55. Any 8-inch bowl can flake near the rim.

2. Flakes

A flake refers to a thin layer that splits from the glass—most often near a rim or on a deep miter (S 54). The flake will feel uneven to the touch. The damage may occur on either the inside or outside of the rim. Running your finger around the rim may not always detect a flake. If you grasp the edge between forefinger and thumb and move slowly around the rim, you can detect the flakes.

On a bowl (S 55), a vase (S 56), or a piece with a straight rim (S 57) the flake appears near the rim. Look for flakes on the lip, base, or handles of jugs (P 58). The removal or replacement of a stopper on a decanter (C 59) may cause a flake on the inside neck. Drinking glasses flake easily on the rim and the base (S 60).

S 56. Careful handling of this ll-inch vase has prevented flakes on the rim and base.

57. The clear rims of this two-piece mayonnaise signed Hawkes would quickly show any flakes if not mint.

C 59. The careful removal of stoppers prevents flaking inside the neck as in this 11-inch decanter.

P 58. This 11-inch decanter has no flakes on the neck, lip, base, or decorated handle.

S 60. Always check the rims of tumblers for flakes.

3. Bruises

The term "bruises" describes a multitude of tiny scratches that produce a cloudiness on clear spots in the pattern of tumblers, trays (S 61), jugs (C 62), comports (C 63), or any large, covered jars for crackers (P 64) or tobacco. Any good cut glass shows a sensitivity to scratching when placed on an uneven or slightly rough surface. Collectors and dealers call these scratches "age" or "wear" marks as they indicate usage over a period of time. Counterfeiters have placed such marks on new European glass or reproductions of old cut glass so as to pass the pieces off as old.

S 61. The heavy cutting of this 14-inch tray will prevent bruises from showing.

C 62. Any bruise will show on the base of this 12-inch jug signed by Averbeck Cut Glass Company.

C 63. The single star on the foot of this 7-inch comport will show if it has bruises.

P 64. Careful handling as with this large cracker jar has prevented bruises where lid joins the jar and on the base.

Flower frogs or holders will leave bruise marks on the inside of any bowls if used for floral arrangements. Companies cut more ornate patterns to keep bruises from showing, adding more minor motifs, such as cane (P 65) and crosshatching (C 66). A magnifying glass clearly shows the depth of the bruises. A skilled repairman can remove deep bruises if they mar the beauty of a piece. Otherwise, let the bruises remain as evidence of authenticity.

P 65. Heavy cutting on this 11-inch by 8-inch tray prevented bruises.

C 66. Minute cutting of crosshatching protected this 12 by 8-inch tray from bruising.

P 67. This 10-inch comport has a clear foot that shows no fractures.

S 68. Always look at the rim and the base of a tumbler for fractures.

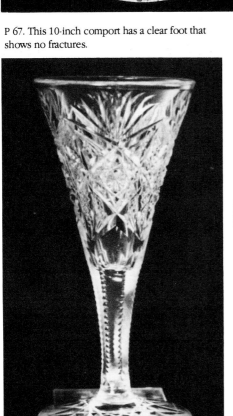

S 69. A sherry glass can fracture easily on the rim and foot if used frequently.

P 70. Excellent care has prevented any fracture on the neck of this 14-inch decanter.

P 71. This 14-inch vase has no fractures on the clear rim.

4. Fractures

Fractures—a myriad of tiny cracks—result from accidentally hitting two pieces of glass together or against a hard surface. You can see those that mar the beauty of a piece. Look for fractures on the top or bottom of a footed piece (P 67), the rim or base of a tumbler (S 68), stemware (S 69), decanters (P 70), or vases (P 71), to name a few. Examine any piece that regularly comes in close contact with another, such as a jug (C 72) with tumblers or the dome of covered cheese or butter with plate (S 73).

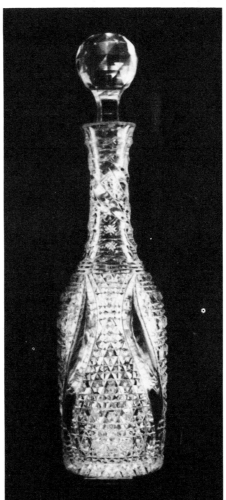

S 72. The care of this 11-inch jug has prevented any fractures.

S 73. Fractures frequently occur on the rim of the dome of a butter when replaced carelessly on the plate.

In brilliant cut glass, almost any piece can develop a fracture and reduce the value. A repairman cannot remove a fracture, and any such attempt will only crack the glass more.

5. Crush Points

Crush points refer to a pin-point, white dot that appears on the surface of cut glass. A strong blow to the piece causes the crush point. When a repairman tries to polish out the point, the glass will fracture more or break. Unless you look closely, you will not see this small, white speck. It can appear at any place on any piece of cut glass. If you own a piece with a crush point, ignore it; but watch for any when you buy glass.

6. Cracks

A crack designates an actual cleavage in the glass, whether or not you can feel it. Brilliant cut glass cracks when exposed to extreme temperatures of hot and cold. For some unknown reason, a piece can crack right in a protective cabinet.

Sometimes cracks follow a deep miter on a large plate (S 74) and make detection almost impossible. Drinking glasses crack along the top edge. Applied handles break at the point of application or nearby. Simply trying to remove a tight stopper or "dropping" it into the neck of a decanter causes a crack.

To locate a crack, examine a piece under a strong light and check with a magnifying glass. Look at both the outside and the inside where possible. A crack on an uncut surface usually shows up clearly, but one on a heavily cut pattern may challenge you. Any time a piece has a large chip or flake, examine these spots for a crack. Ask the owner to thump a piece that ordinarily rings. A flat tone indicates a crack. Remember, shallow pieces ring only slightly.

S 74. Careful handling has prevented any cracks along the deep miters of this 9-inch plate.

S 75. This 8-inch tall comport contains the original silver rim.

C 76. This decorated rim on a cream to a set verifies it as original.

C 77. This small jewel box contained chips under the silver rim in Pattern #2002 signed J. Hoare.

On any silver fitting always look for a hallmark (S 75). With no hallmark or lack of decoration on the silver (C 76), someone may have added the silver rim later to hide chips or cracks. Any time a silver rim appears on a piece that ordinarily would not have one or in places that chip easily, get suspicious.

Cracks often develop if a professional silversmith does not remove the rim for replating. Especially look at hinged boxes, such as jewel (C 77) or handkerchief. Most silversmiths prefer to remove a rim from the glass for replating or else will give you specific directions on how to do the job.

Never knowingly buy a cracked piece unless you can do so very cheaply. A few collectors will buy a rare shape or pattern with s slight crack to display only in a cabinet.

7. Heat Checks

When the gaffer applied the handles to an item, he tried to keep the piece and the handle exactly the same temperature. He usually applied the lower end first so the upper part has more time to cool. If the handle cools too quickly, a tiny, white line or heat check appears where he attached the upper part.

Some believe a handle will break at heat check, but we have never seen one that did. Certainly a heat check weakens a handle, and most dealers and collectors admit such a flaw reduces the value of a piece.

Before you buy any article with a handle, look inside at the spot where the handle joins the body, as in a jug (C 78). The glass should appear clear. Put you finger on the outside where the handle joins the shape at the top, and you can see the heat check more clearly. If you find a heat check, buy at your own risk.

Ocassionally, handles do not adhere completely to the body of the piece. In fact you can put the tip of a fingernail between the handle and the body, as in a basket (C 79) or a nappy. The handle may crack or break off where it did not adhere to the body.

8. Sick Glass

Sick includes the following three types of damages. A cloudy or frosted look may appear inside of a piece. The acidity in vinegar, wine, rum, salt, or perfume causes a chemical reaction that oxidizes the inner surface. Some will insist that this oxidation resulted from too high an alkaline content in the glass batch.

If you put water or liquid in a piece with this type of sick, the white disappears until the glass dries. A little oil, wax cleaner, or a nonstick cooking spray will also

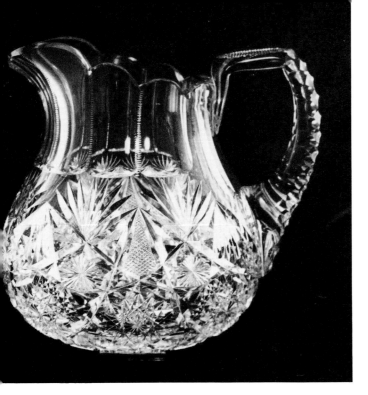

78. This 7-inch tall jug has no heat check on the handle.

C 79. The handles on the 6-inch basket clearly adhere to the bowl.

clear the sick temporarily unless you use too much. Then the inside of the decanter or cologne looks as if someone washed it but failed to dry it. Avoid buying this type of sick as it will not wash out. A repairman can remove it by grinding or with acid, but he person will not guarantee the job as permanent.

Another type of sick may wash out if it builds from a residue in the bottom of decanters, bottles, or vases not properly cleaned. You can remove some of the deposits by soaking the glass in a false teeth cleaner. Never use soap for a dish washer—much too strong. You may need to soak the piece for several days and then loosen the residue with cotton on a long swab stick.

In the third type of sick glass, the crystals separate as a result of imperfect fusing of the metal or too short a time for annealing. When you hold the piece against a strong light, you can see a web of minute fissures. A few think that the glass will eventually shatter. Mr. Gerould, an old-time cutter, referred to this type glass as crazed, but he didn't think it would explode. Never buy it no matter how cheap. All types of sickness may develop in one piece of glass or perhaps only one.

REPAIRED GLASS

Whether or not repairs show depends on the size, the type of damage, and the skill of the craftsman. Some collectors may refuse to buy a chipped piece, so dealers have it repaired. Other dealers will sell the piece as is, and let the buyer arrange for any repairs. Unless you have become skilled in determining the possibility of a good repair, let the dealer handle the job. Repairs consist of four types: re-cut, re-style, restore, or re-assemble.

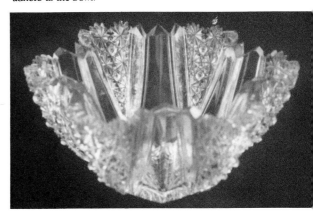

L 80. A comparison points to a cut rim on this crimped bowl signed Hawkes.

Re-cut

Re-cutting protects the damaged item from chipping or flaking more, but any buyer of cut glass needs to learn how to visualize the resulting repairs.

Rims. Tumblers and stemware have a rounded bulge immediately under the rim caused by fire polishing. In reducing the rim to remove a chip or a flake, the repairman cuts away part or all of this inside curve. Always feel inside for this curve under the rim. A deep repair of the rim may also reduce the height somewhat (L 80) when compared to another duplicate piece (P 81). If the rim of a piece looks uneven, place it upside down on an even surface and see if it rocks. A rocking piece indicates an uneven repair. The original craftsman rounded the rim after cutting with fire polishing, so a sharp or flat edge indicates a repair. Ask the seller about a possible repair.

P 81. An 8-inch bowl in Russian and signed Hawkes in original form.

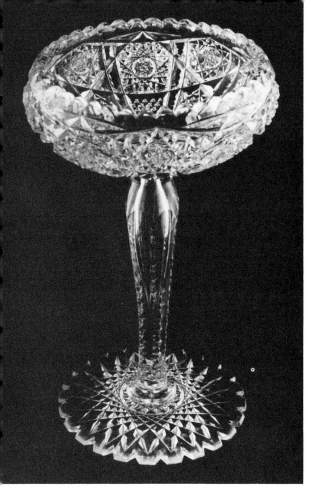

C 82. A sawtooth foot on a 9.5-inch comport needs special care to prevent a scollop from getting nicked.

C 84. This 11-inch jug has an original, stubby lip.

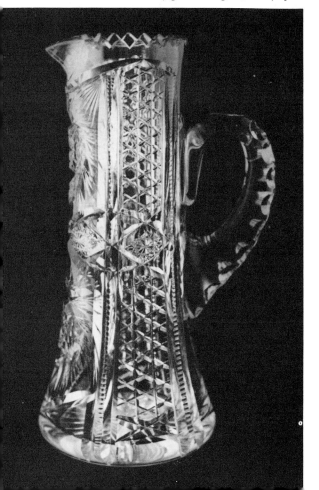

C 83. The pattern on this 10-inch plate would prevent any repairs on the rim.

Foot: Items with a foot, such as a vase or comport (C 82) may get nicked on the base. The original craftsman rounded the edge of the base, so a perpendicular one suggests a trimming. Check the star on the under foot to see if it comes too close to the edge or looks uneven.

Borders: Most patterns of cut glass leave a clear border between the rim and the pattern, but several companies, such as Pitkins & Brooks, left no border (C 83). With no border, the repair cuts into the pattern. A sharp tooth instead of a rounded one or a scalloped rim possibly suggests a recut.

Look for irregular spacing between scollops. With extensive damage, the repairman may need to replace a scalloped, sawtooth rim with a straight sawtooth one.

Miters: Occasionally deep miters get damaged. The removal of a chip or flake may cause a dip or widening of the miter. You can often see the irregularity or the cutting marks or feel it by running your fingers up and down the miters.

Producers of cut glass blanks maintained the same thickness on the neck of a jug, carafe, decanter, or bowl, to name a few. Differences in thickness may result from a repair. Some jugs (C 84) originally contained a stubby lip, but too little spout or one thicker on one side should arouse questions. Recognizing differences in polishing requires more experience. You can notice a slight grayness in a pattern when compared to brightness of an original polish.

Learn to recognize these inconsistencies and then decide whether to buy. Do not hesitate to buy a piece with a good re-cut, but with re-styling, stop and think.

2. Re-Styling

A repair person may get a piece so badly damaged, he must re-style. Some adaptations of damaged glass, however, challenge the imagination. A carafe with a broken neck became a rose globe. The unbroken base of a cylindrical vase sold as wine coaster two inches deep. A repairman, no doubt at the request of the owner, removed the handle from a catsup (L85). Handles removed from a basket became a bonbon (L86), and a two handled nappy (S 87) became one without handles (L88). The removal of the top and the bottom of a mug (L 89) produced an odd piece found in a flea market.

L 85. A repairman has removed the handle from this catsup.

L 86. The converted 10 by 4-inch basket underwent removal of handles.

S 87. A 6-inch, two-handled nappy by Marshall Field & Company in #72016 pattern.

L 88. The same two-handled nappy with the broken handles removed.

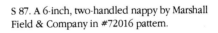

L 89. A mug with the rim and base removed.

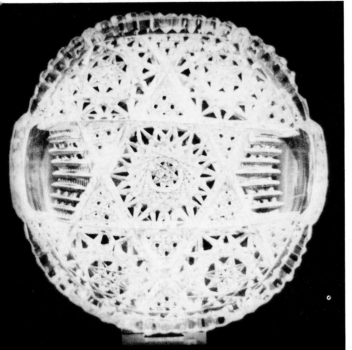

L 91. A cut glass candelabra converted to a lamp.

L 92. A re-glued 6-inch nappy in Elfin by Hoare.

L 90. A 12-inch punch bowl married to a silver
Pairpoint base.

Conversions take other forms. When a silver base fit the top of a punch bowl, the collector married them (L 90). The cut glass base of a candelabra converted to a lamp with the addition of a frame, shade, and prisms (L 91). Any time the shape of a cut glass item looks a little odd or not quite right, carefully examine it as a fanciful conversion.

3. Restoring

To restore means to return the piece to the nearly original condition. Today, expert repairmen constantly accomplish this task so well the piece retains 95% of its value. During the Brilliant Period companies housed a repair shop. If pieces became slightly damaged before shipment, they went to the repair room. In case of slight damages, the cutter restored the piece and shipped it to the customer as mint.

Before a repairman undertakes to restore a piece of glass, he studies it carefully so he can duplicate the original. Restoration means repeating the same pattern as nearly as possibly by recutting the damage. The width of the miters and characteristic notching match. He carefully polishes the item to remove all whiteness from cutting. Such repair people constantly experiment with new tools and test skills to improve the art of restoration. Never hesitate to buy a piece with a good restoration.

4. Re-Assembling

Repairs of broken glass have become very sophisticated. New glues enable a repairman to re-assemble broken pieces into the original shape (L92). Not only can you barely see the glued parts, but some pieces will even ring. Only a strong light reveals the repairs. Most prove waterproof for regular use (L 9 3). If you feel sentimental about a broken piece, this new glue may save it for you.

SPECIAL CHECKS

Two-part pieces need special checking for mating and not for marriage. Two-part pieces include punch bowls, mayonnaise, domed cheese and butter, or various sets.

1. Mate or Marry

Mate means to match two-part pieces exactly (P 94). In a marriage two similar shapes get put together as in a lamp (L 95). Both the major and minor motifs must appear in the same arrangement. A jug and tumblers must match (C 96).

93. A re-glued 8-inch bowl in Jupiter, F. B.
Tinker.

P 94. A 15-inch punch bowl where foot and bowl
match.

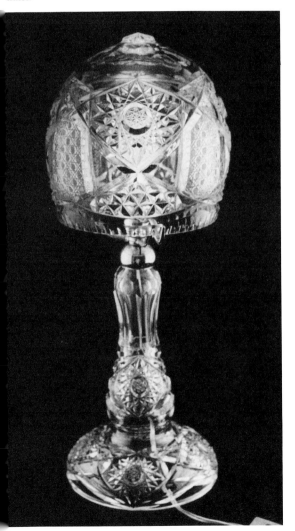

95. A small lamp where foot and shade do not
match.

C 96. A set in Mignon Pattern by Libbey where jug
and tumblers mate.

C 97. The cheeze dome and underplate must match.

L 98. The original lamp and the one with the replaced globe in Dorflinger's Strawberry Diamond Pattern.

Underplates in a set have a high casualty rate. The underplate of a mayonnaise must match the bowl. Other mating includes the dome and underplate of a cheese or butter (C 97) or dome and base of a pair of lamps (L 98). The collector arranged to restore a broken dome on one of the two lamps. This required blowing a matching blank and cutting the identical pattern.

2. Stoppers and Lids

Stoppers frequently get broken or misplaced. The Americans produced stoppers in standard sizes and shapes for special pieces. A stopper with a thick neck went with a cologne (P 99) or a rum jug. The decanter (P 100) and oil used stoppers with long slender necks. A stopper with a design should match the pattern on the piece (P 101).

To check the stopper as the original one, look for a number on the flat bottom or the side and see if it matches the one on the outside or inside of the neck. Not all pieces, however, contained numbered stoppers. The wrong stopper rocks back and forth in the neck, goes in too deeply or not far enough (L 102). Remember, a ground stopper needs a ground neck. Make sure that the lid design matches that of the base in a puff box (C 103) or a cracker jar (P 104).

By this time you may think you will never become an astute buyer, but you will. Surprisingly, when you look at a piece of cut glass, these warnings will flash through your mind. Pat yourself on the back each time you successfully use them. Very soon they will become almost automatic. Now you need to take another step forward and become informed about signatures.

P 100. A decanter signed Hoare contains the correct stopper.

P 99. A 7-inch cologne with the correct stopper.

P 101. The cut stopper matches the decanter in this piece signed Libbey.

L 102. The stopper goes in too far on the oil, and the decorated stopper does not match the pattern or fit the neck in the Chelsea Pattern by Hawkes.

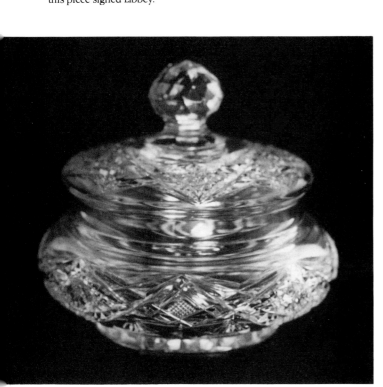

C 103. The lid matches the jar in this 6-inch piece.

P 104. The lid matches the cracker jar in this signed Hoare, 7.5-inch piece.

Chapter 3
Facts About Signatures

P 105. A leaf-shaped bonbon in the original Russian pattern patented by Hawkes.

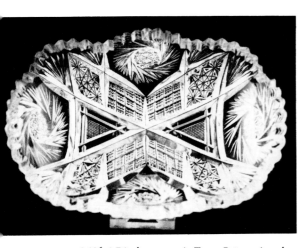

S 106. A 7-inch spooner in Topaz Pattern signed by Pitkin and Brooks in a standard design.

P 107. A crimped bowl in Pinto, an ornate pattern by Pitkin and Brooks, but not signed.

In the early years of the Brilliant Period, the growing competition between cut glass companies developed a problem in ownership of patterns. Any company could cut the simple, public-domain patterns brought from Europe, but American designs proved more ornate and popular. At the large companies a master craftsman created these patterns, but small companies operated without a designer. So these small companies copied the patterns of larger ones. Because of such unauthorized copying, the large companies looked for ways to protect their patterns.

PATTERN PROTECTION

A number of companies decided that securing a patent on a pattern would protect it. This seemed the quickest and most likely solution to the problem.

1. Patents

When a master craftsman designed a unique pattern, he applied for a patent. As soon as the government granted the patent, the designer assigned the ownership of the pattern to the company for which he worked. The records show that Phillip McDonald received the first patent on the Russian Pattern, June 20, 1882, and assigned it to Hawkes (P 105). We could find no earlier date in the patent records.

To copy such a registered pattern within dates designated infringed on the copyright. Copyrights covered varying periods of time: three and one-half, seven, or fourteen years. When the patent expired, the pattern went into public domain, and any company could cut it.

Rather than wait for the patent to expire, small shops broke the patent by changing one or two small parts of the design. They could replace a bit of crosshatching with a cane diamond. This slight change in the pattern went unnoticed by the casual buyer but not by the owner of the patent. This breaking of patents caused the large companies to find a better means of protecting a pattern, such as with signatures.

2. Copyrighted Signatures

Several companies decided that an acid-etched signature on the cut glass provided a positive means of identifying the company of origin. So in 1895, both Hawkes and Libbey announced they would place a signature on all of their glass. Other companies, such as T. B. Clark & Company and J. D. Bergen Company, also used a signature.

While a number of companies signed pieces, they delayed getting a copyright on it. J. Hoare & Company did not copyright the signature until May 12, 1900, although he stated he had used it since 1895. Hawkes did not register his signature until March 3, 1903, but he reported he had used it since July, 1890. 0. F. Egginton Company registered the signature on January 23, 1906, seven years after he organized the company. Tuthill did not copyright his signature until 1919.

When companies first began to sign cut glass, they chose only the finest pieces. Pitkin and Brooks frankly stated in their catalogs that they signed all quality pieces (S 106); however a signature appears on this one and not on the ornate piece (P 107). Hawkes signed a relish in a simple pattern (S 108), possibly from the early years, but this ornate piece has no signature (P 109).

Do keep in mind that these examples represent exceptions. In a majority of patterns, the companies did sign the glass. Signatures, never-the-less, did created considerable confusion.

S 108. A 6-inch relish in a simple pattern and signed by Hawkes.

SIGNATURE CONFUSION

Although a signature offered a positive identification of the source, they did create some confusion. You can eliminate much of this confusion by understanding how the situations developed.

1. Omission of Signature

Most agree that the lowest paid and normally the least responsible employee of the glass company stamped the signature. Understandably the employee may have carelessly skipped a piece now and then when stamping hundreds. Of two identical celeries purchased at the same time, only one has the Clark signature (S 110).

P 109. An 8-inch tall, footed bowl in pattern #1283 by Hawkes but not signed.

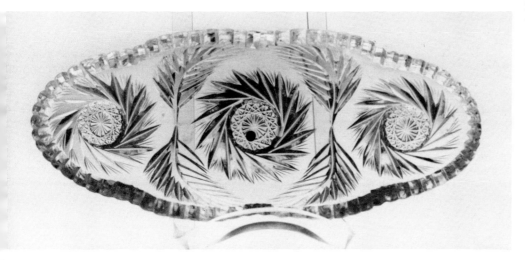

S 110. An 11-inch celery in Ideal Pattern signed by Clark. The mate has no signature.

P 111. An 11-inch tall jug in Puritana Pattern in shape Libbey kept for own use but not signed.

P 112. A rum jug, not signed, but in a shape used almost exclusively by Libbey.

Libbey and Hawkes continued to advertise in magazines that they signed every piece and urged buyers to look for the signature. The Libbey factory supposedly never sold two shape of blanks to other companies: a jug with an odd lip (P 111) and a squat rum one (P 112). A collector owns such a rum jug signed Sinclaire, and the Canadian company, Grundy-Clapperton Company, used it in the Classic Pattern. Clapperton apprenticed with the Libbey Glass Company for ten years. Neither of the above Libbey shapes has a signature. With no signature, you use other sources of identification, such as old catalogs.

2. Altered Signatures

Even though companies registered a signature, they simplified it in actual use. H. C. Fry Glass Company patented a scripted name on a shield, but he signed his glass only with the scripted "Fry" (P 113). Very late in the Brilliant Period he block lettered the "Fry." Between 1896 and 1919, Libbey used five signatures (See Appendix), but the company used the one with a sword throughout the Brilliant Period (P 114).

P 113. An 8-inch bowl in Lewis Pattern by Fry with scripted name signature.

P 114. A 7-inch bowl with the Libbey sword signature.

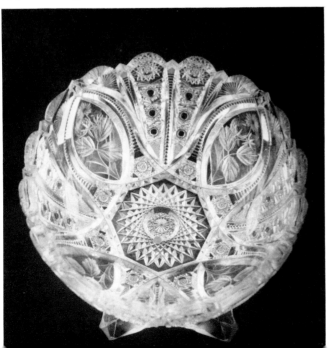

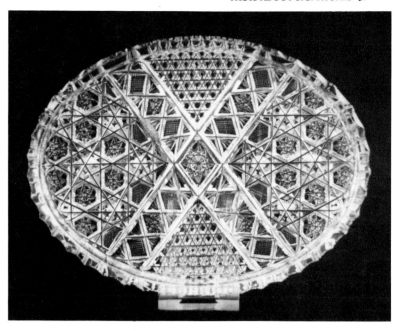

S 115. A 9-inch, square dish in Corinthian Pattern by Libbey with the sword signature in one corner and the eagle one off center.

C 116. A 7-inch, butter fluff tray signed with the 1853 signature by Hoare.

C 117. An 8-inch bowl in the Limoges Pattern and signed with Hoare's Corning signature.

In 1893, at the Columbian Exposition held in Chicago, Libbey sold several souvenirs, such as a pottery shaker and hatchet that contained a new signature, an eagle inside a double circle. A magazine advertisement later stated that this signature would appear on all Libbey glass. Recently, a collector showed us a square Libbey dish that contained two signatures: the sword one in the corner, and the eagle-centered one etched a little off center (S 115).

J. Hoare and Sons used two signatures. One included the date "1853" across the center of double circles. This date refers to the year he started his glass company in the United States (C 116). The other signature substitutes Corning for the date. This later signature replaced the dated one when he moved his cutting shop to Corning (C 117).

J. D. Bergen signed some pieces with the two, intersecting globes (P 118), but ordinarily he used a scripted name (C 119). So first learn the most used version and then the occasional one.

P 118. A 5-inch bonbon signed with Bergen's two globes signature.

C 119. A 7-inch plate in Golf Pattern signed with a scripted Bergen.

P 120. A covered butter and plate, 6-inches tall, in Seminole Pattern, signed Maple City Glass Company with a flat-base, maple leaf.

3. Similar Signatures

Similarity in signatures, likewise, caused confusion. The Maple City Glass Company signed with a flat-based, maple leaf (P 120). Clark copyrighted a full maple leaf, but we have never seen any other signature but the scripted name (C 121). Later Clark bought the Maple City Glass Company. Of two identical bowls, one has the leaf of Maple City and the other the scripted Clark signature (C 122).

Libbey received a copyright for a signature of a star in a circle to place on mold-blown blanks. We have seen only one piece of glass cut on such a molded blank (S 123). Some confuse this trademark with that of Straus (P 124).

C 121. An 8-inch vase in Jacqueminot Pattern and signed with the scripted Clark.

C 122. An 8-inch bowl in Shelocton Pattern by Maple City but another in identical pattern signed Clark.

S 123. A 6-inch tall covered butter and plate signed with a circled S indicating a mold-blown blank from Libbey.

P 124. A 16-inch tall, punch bowl with two parts signed Straus, an S in a circle.

S 125. A goblet signed by Almy & Thomas and Averbeck, in Radium Pattern by the latter.

4. Double Usage

At times some retailers and wholesalers used their own trademark in conjunction with that of the company that produced the glass. A goblet signed by Averbeck Cut Glass Company also has an Almy and Thomas signature (S 125). Van Heusen, Charles & Company served as agents for Libbey and did no cutting. Yet they signed glass (S 126).

Canadian companies frequently added the agent's signature to that of the producer. Recently, a dealer showed us a wine (C 127) signed in block letters by both Birks, a Canadian company, and Hawkes. On a tumbler the signature consisted of the block-lettered "Birks" on top and beneath the regular Hawkes trefoil (S 128).

S 126. A 7-inch plate signed Van Heusen, Charles Company.

C 127. A wine signed by Birks, a Canadian company, and Hawkes.

S 128. A tumbler signed Birks in block letters and the regular trefoil signature in Oxford Pattern by Hawkes.

S 129. One of two 7-inch plates, one contained a Hawkes signature and the other a Sinclaire one.

P 130. A presentation punch bowl signed Libbey and pattern later added to the regular line.

In another type of double usage, two different companies signed the same pattern. Both Sinclaire and Egginton designed patterns for Hawkes. When they decided to organize their own company, Hawkes permitted them to take the patterns they designed with them.

Until Hawkes exhausted the supply on hand, he and the others signed the patterns (S 129).

5. The Signed and Unsigned

From time to time companies produced presentation pieces on special order. The company etched a personal inscription on the piece rather than a signature (P 130). On occasion the company then would add such patterns to the general line and sign them (P 131).

Periodically organizations ordered pieces as souvenirs for their convention. A souvenir for the Daughters of the Nile, a lodge, contained the symbol of the organization, a simitar and the name Zenobia. Libbey also added its trademark. We have seen several of these Zenobia souvenirs (S 132).

P 131. A presentation punch bowl signed Libbey and added to the regular line.

S 132. A 5-inch saucer cut as a convention souvenir for Daughters of the Nile has both Libby signature and symbol of the organization.

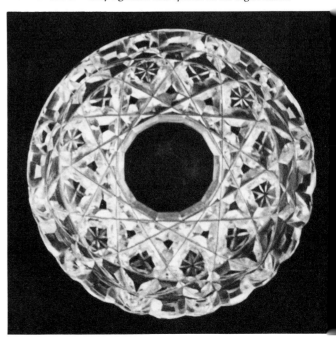

Color-cut-to-clear glass rarely gets signed. We have seen a decanter in ruby-cut-to-clear signed Hawkes in the Chrysanthemum Pattern. A collector has a loving cup in ruby-cut-to-blue-to-clear in the Crystal City Pattern signed Hoare. Fry and Libbey, on rare occasions, signed color-cut-to-clear glass.

5. Forgeries

Because a signature adds value to cut glass, forgers saw a way to make money. Some forgers have approached dealers and offered to sign any piece with any signature. At first the counterfeiter used an electric needle to copy the signature. Such signatures you can feel with your fingernail. The forger today uses a rubber stamp and acid.

Fortunately for the collector most of the forgers have not studied the signatures. One block lettered the "Irving" rather than scripted it (S 133). A collector showed us a bowl in the Heart Pattern by Pitkin and Brooks, a very well-known design, but it contained a scripted Clark signature done with an electric needle (C 134). On a modern ashtray cut with panels someone scripted "Hawkes" on it (L 135). Knowing the signatures of the companies will protect you against forgery.

S 133. A six-inch plate in Zella Pattern by Irving Cut Glass Co. Inc. has the signature block lettered.

L 135. A modern ashtray signed with a scripted Hawkes.

C 134. An 8-inch bowl in Heart Pattern by Pitkin and Brooks has the scripted Clark done with an electric needle.

C 136. A cologne signed Bonnet.

S 137. A sugar and cream with Diamond in block letters on the flat of the handle.

P 138. A 13-inch jug with CH on the flat of the handle.

7. Unidentified Signatures

Over the last few years collectors and dealers have sent us sketches of unidentified signatures. One sketch has REEDER in an oval and another MB Co, possibly Baker Company. A person sent a different signature of Hobbs, Brockunier & Co., B H C in a clover leaf. A truly ornate one consists of KOB Co.

A collector wrote that the Bonnet signature belonged to the Bonnet Company but could give no further details. Since then we found another piece signed Bonnet (C 136) in Washington state, possibly a Canadian company. C. F. Monore did sign some of the cut glass with the block letters: C. F. M. Co. "Diamond" in block letters appears on the handle of a sugar and cream (S 137). The top of the handle on a jug contains the block letters "CH" (P 138). The signature of Regnier in block letters on a banner appeared in the center of a relish dish.

We have received two different signatures with the initials TMJ: one shows the initials below an anchor and the other placed the letters in a heart. One collector suggested that the signature belonged to the T. M. James Jewelry Company in Kansas.

These numerous, unknown signatures may have a logical explanation. Cutters who operated shops in barns and basements followed the lead of large companies and signed their glass. The small operators saw no need to copyright a signature; consequently they could change one at any time.

If you collect signatures, then buy the piece with the unknown one. In spite of this confusion involving signatures, collectors and dealers search diligently for them. A recognized signature identifies the source of a piece and thereby increases the value.

THE SEARCH FOR SIGNATURES

Nothing compares to the excitement of finding a signature on a piece of glass you thought unsigned. Your excitement increases when you recognize company trademarks.

1. Etching the Signature

All companies acid-etched the signature. An employee pressed a rubber stamp with a trademark on a pad saturated with a special, acid formula. Then he pressed the stamp firmly on a clear spot in the glass pattern so that the acid adhering to the rubber stamp would etch the signature.

P 139. Wear has erased part of the Clark signature on this 12-inch tray in the Mars Pattern.

C 140. A 12-inch plate with a faint Clark signature.

2. Discovery Methods

Some signatures truly challenge discovery for a number of reasons: weak acid, worn stamp, or blurred double stamping. Usage may particially erase a signature (P 139). The very small size or an inconspicuous location makes a signature difficult to find. Often you miss a faint Clark (C 140) or Egginton signature. Fry, Libbey (S 141), and Pitkin and Brooks (C 142) have a strong signature. Even though you do not see a signature right away, keep looking especially at different times.

Dealers and collectors use various methods to locate these signatures. One dealer uses a black light to find the evasive signature. Some collectors found a florescent lamp or ordinary table lamp sufficient. Late afternoon sunlight worked for another person. Another recommended a flashlight with a plastic rim. No matter what type of light you use or what search method you employ, rotate the piece until the light reflects a mirror-like surface.

Speaking of elusive signatures, a short time ago an auction house discovered a Libbey signature on a piece of glass cut in the most ornate pattern of the so described "Expanding Star" (P 143). We have found signatures on pieces in a simpler design of this pattern by Gowans, Kent & Company, Limited and Roden Brothers, both of Canada.

C 142. A middle size sugar and cream on a foot with a strong Pitkin and Brooks signature.

S 141. A 7-inch bowl with a strong Libbey signature.

P 143. A handled nappy in the descriptive name, "Expanding Star" Pattern. At a recent auction a piece in the exact pattern contained a Libbey signature.

S 144. Six punch cups have a Fry signature in the center and six on the rim under the foot in Orient Pattern.

C 145. Hoare signed this 8-inch, low bowl slightly off center.

SIGNATURE PLACEMENT

The etcher might place a signature in almost any blank spot on a piece. At times the customary space would not accommodate the entire signature, so he stamped i over or along a miter.

Generally, companies placed the signature in one particular spot; others varied the location even on pieces in a set. Of a dozen Fry punch cups, six have the signature on the inside center and the others under the foot near the rim (S 144). So study these basic and unique placements of signatures.

1. Round Pieces: Bowls, Trays, Plates, Butter Pats

The inside center seems the favorite place for a signature on these items. Hoare usually signed a little off center (C 145). Libbey often signed in a space near the sawtooth rim (C 146). Sinclaire and Tuthill (P 147) signed on the inside corner o oval trays.

C 146. Libbey signed this 8-inch, square bowl near the top rim.

C 147. Tuthill signed this 10-inch tray in a clear spot near the top edge.

C 148. Hoare signed this 13-inch tall decanter on the under base near the rim.

2. Container: Bottles, Carages, Decanters, Flower Centers

Signatures on these items appear most often on the base near the edge (C 148). Odd locations include: Libbey where the neck and flute join the body (P 149), Fry on the top rim of a carafe, Straus inside the neck of a carafe (C 150), Fry on the facet of a neck ring of a decanter, and Libbey under the extended rim of a wine decanter.

P 149. Libbey signed this carafe in Ellsmere Pattern at the bottom of a neck flute.

C 150. Straus signed this carafe inside the neck.

C 151. Hawkes signed this 5.5-inch puff box inside both parts. Pattern listed as #1250.

P 152. A cracker jar signed Hawkes on the under edge of the base.

C 153. On an 8-inch, covered bonbon, Tuthill signed the top edge of both pieces.

3. Lidded Pieces: Jars and Boxes

Most companies used the regular location on boxes, such as puff, jewel, or handkerchief—inside the lid or bowl—sometimes both (C 151). Some companies signed on the under rim of the base, a place used for tobacco and cracker jars (P 152). On a covered bonbon Tuthill signed on the edge of each rim (C 153).

4. Handled Pieces: Jugs, Bowls, Cups, Spooners

Most companies signed these pieces in four, basic locations: Libbey on the flat of the handle (C 154), Hoare somewhere inside center (P 155), Sinclare on the under rim of the base (P 156), and Hawkes on a clear spot directly under the handle (P 157). Clark signed more often on the under rim of the base

Dealers and collectors have reported finding signatures in odd places: Tuthill and Libbey under the lip of a jug, Pitkin and Brooks on the side of a sugar and cream, Wright chose to sign both the flat of the handle and the under base on a sugar and cream. Egginton etched the signature on the upper, outside rim near the handle of a punch cup.

5. Footed Pieces: Comports, Wines, Decanters, Cruets

Footed pieces mostly have the signature on the top edge of the foot or the under rim. If accessible, the signature appeared inside center. Clark usually signed under the rim of the foot, and Hawkes and Libbey favored the top edge. Both Tuthill and Taylor Brothers chose a space between the rays of the single star on the base. On a comport Libbey chose the stem, a very odd exception.

6. Tubular Pieces: Tumblers, Spooners, Vases

With tumblers and spooners you find the signature either inside the center or on the under edge of the base. Libbey signed identical whiskey tumblers one on the under edge of the base and the other on the inside center. With another tumbler Libbey placed the signature on a clear square at the side near the base.

7. Other Shapes

So the placement of signatures varies with the company and with the shape. A napkin ring has the signature inside near the rim, on the rim itself, or on the outside in a clear spot near the rim. Baskets contain a signature on the inside center, on the under rim of the base, and under or on top of a handle. A signature appears on the globe and the foot of a lamp in a clear spot near the rim.

Hawkes signed a pair of candelabras on the stem under the branches, on salt and pepper shakers in the center of the base, and on a saucer across a miter. A knife rest may show the signature on either a facet of the knob or on the bar between. A collector found a Fry signature on a glass facet of the handle on a ladle. Sinclaire signed a clock on the back near the top. Libbey's signature on candlesticks appeared on the top rim of the foot.

Never give up searching for a signature. One more look may discover it in a regular or an odd place. Most dealers and collectors mark the signature—especially if difficult to discover—with a small dot.

C 154. Libbey signed on the flat of the handle in this 7.5-inch fern.

P 155. Hoare signed off center in this 18-inch tray.

P 156. Sinclaire signed on the under rim of the base on this 10-inch loving cup.

P 157. This 6-inch jug Hawkes signed under the handle.

ALTERNATE IDENTIFICATIONS

A number of companies used other means of identifying their products, some permanent and others not so permanent.

1. Paper Labels

Dorflinger relied mostly on a paper label (P 158). David Dorflinger affirmed that after the factory closed John Dorflinger reproduced the two labels of Dorflinger and placed them on pieces he recognized as cut by Christian Dorflinger. The carafe (C 159) has a block letter "Dorflinger" on the silver neck. David also confirmed that Dorflinger acid etched pieces with the same designs as the two on the paper stickers but very rarely.

2. Silver Hallmarks

Most silver mountings on cut glass contained a hallmark from the company that produced it. Dorflinger block lettered the name on the silver, and Pairpoint used a capital P in a diamond (C 160). On later pieces Pairpoint did spell out the name. The short time Hawkes mounted the silver on pieces, he block lettered the name. When a glass company contracted for another to provide the silver fitting, that company used its own hallmark. Always check the hallmark to give it at least a silver identification.

3. Liners

A number of cut glass items, such as flower pots, urns, and ferns came with a metal liner (S 161). Union Glass Company, Shotten Cut Glass Company, and Pairpoint Corporation put their name on liners. Loss of liner meant loss of the identification. An original liner, especially a sterling silver one (C 162) or metal (S 163) adds value. Recently, a dealer gave us the address of a person who reproduces liners in silver plate. These carry no identification of source.

No search proves more profitable than finding an identification for the cut glass you already own or that you plan to buy. A very important part of buying and collecting involves speaking the language.

P 158. A pair of candlesticks contain the original paper label of Dorflinger.

C 159. Dorflinger appears in block letters on the silver neck of this carafe.

S 161. A 7.5-inch fern in #75563 by Marshall Field has a liner.

C 160. These 9-inch candlesticks have Pairpoint on the silver base.

S 163. This 8-inch flower holder in Dover Pattern by Pairpoint has Union Cut Glass Company on the liner, possibly a marriage.

S 162. This 7.5-inch fern contains a sterling silver lining.

Chapter 4

Decorating the Blank

S 164. A 10.5-inch cake tray with straight miters.

Speaking the language of cut glass enables you to describe a piece so that a deal or collector can visualize it. Although the Americans relied on the same decoratin processes for cut glass as the Europeans—cutting, engraving, silver fitting, ar coloring—they made the piece more decorative. So the Americans developed ne words to describe these changes. As a collector you want to learn these America terms which will help you describe any pattern. Begin with the geometric motif

GEOMETRIC MOTIFS

A geometric motif forms an individual feature of a pattern or design cut on a gla blank. The craftsman named these geometric motifs so as to describe a pattern. Lin formed the basis for the simplest motifs.

1. Line Motifs

Miter: A line, usually v-shaped, referred to a miter. The miters outlined a mot formed a motif, and unified a pattern. Until companies converted to gas and electr power, the craftsman used straight lines for the miters (S 164). This controlle power led to the use of the curved miter (C 165). Many consider that John O'Connor first cut the curved miters. On May 4, 1886, he patented the Parisia Pattern (C 166) for Dorflinger.

Curved miters on some patterns intersected to form a pointed oval (P 167). Th oval also may enclose various motifs (C 168).

Steps: The step motif consisted of horizontal miters in a parallel arrangement (169). The cutter trimmed a neck or base of a decanter with steps (P 170).

C 165. A 7-inch plate signed Hawkes cut with curved miters.

C 166. A 7-inch plate in Parisian Pattern by Dorflinger, first pattern to use curved miters.

C 168. On an 11-inch comport the pointed oval enclosed crosshatched diamonds and star.

P 167. On a 12-inch vase curved miters formed pointed ovals.

169. Hortizontal miters formed steps on this 5-inch cheese dish signed Sinclaire.

P 170. Steps trim the neck and base of this lO-inch decanter with matching stopper.

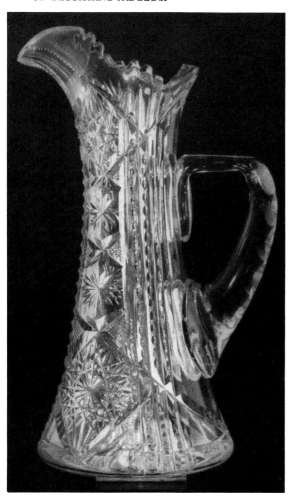

C 171. A 7.5-inch cereal jug signed Hawkes notched the parallel miters.

C 172. On a l0-inch vase the miter notches alternate between simple and complex.

C 173. A 14-inch celery signed Libbey flashes the prongs of a single star.

Notched Miters: This motif notched the edges of the parallel miters, usually vertical, to resemble a string of beads (C 171) so that some refer to it occasionally as "beading." The craftsman cut either simple notches or varied them between short and long. A combination may alternate between the simple and the more complex (C 172).

Feathering: Short, shallow miters outlined a motif for emphasis (C 173). The feathering, also called blaze or fringe, accented a thumbprint, a fan, or points of a star (P 174).

Fan: To form this motif short miters radiated from a focal point to resemble an open fan (S 175). The prongs, always an odd number from three to eleven, depended on the pattern. Fans ordinarily combined with other motifs to form a border or occupy any uncut surface.

To make the motif more ornate, the designer devised new ways to complicate this motif. Some notched the prongs or placed two fans side by side to form a half circle. Four fans of different lengths created a simple motif (C 176), fans between short miters created a fern effect (C 177).

Crosshatching: In crosshatching the cutter filled an area with minute, intersecting lines (C 178). Polishing required a fine brush or acid. Modern European factories often leave this motif an unpolished gray and rough to the touch.

Key: Several companies, such as Libbey and Hawkes, cut a Greek or Roman key for a border. Meriden Cut Glass Company created a key border for the Alhambra Pattern (C 179). A saucer used a swastika for such a border (C 180).

P 174. Flashing accents the hobstar points of a l0-inch bowl.

S 175. Reverse fans decorate this 7-inch plate.

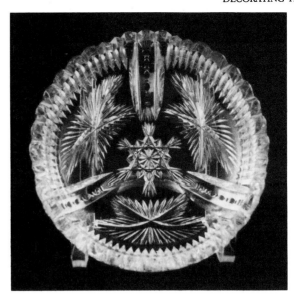

C 176. Fans of different lengths form a motif on this 6-inch nappy.

C 177. A 6.5-inch nappy with fans between the short miters for a fern effect in Fernhurst Pattern by Clark.

C 178. An 11-inch tray signed Libbey in which crosshatched diamonds alternate with hobstars.

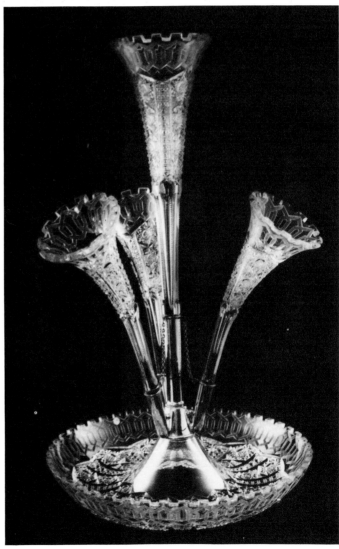

P 179. A 10-inch epergne in Meriden's Alhambra Pattern that shows the Greek key border.

C 180. A 4.5-saucer with a swastika border.

C 181. An 8-inch plate with the Libbey and the NACGMO #5 signatures with varied prongs on the single star.

2. Stars

Of all the geometric motifs, none formed so integral a part of patterns and offere so much variety as the star. The type of star could indicate the period of cutting, th quality of the pattern, and even the producer.

Single Star: This term designated a motif composed of miters that radiated from focal center. Some craftsmen made the miters the same length and other varie them for a scolloped look (C 181). This star decorated the center of bowls or plate the base of a foot on a comport (C 182) or stemware.

C 182. A 7-inch tall comport with a single star on the foot.

P 183. A shooting star motif forms part of the pattern on this 15-inch, tall decanter.

P 184. On this 11-inch tall vase the single star varies the length of the fans for a scolloped effec

C 185. The pattern on a 5-inch, tall ale glass cuts the fans at the border of the single star.

P 186. A 10-inch urn in Empress Pattern by Pitkin & Brooks focuses on one type of sunburst motif.

Shooting Star: This motif widened the space between miters of a single star and inserted fans (P 183). Varying the lengths of the fans formed scallops (P 184). One designer added the fans to the ends of the miters (P 185). The addition of a round center converted the single star to a sunburst motif (P 186).

8-Point Star: Hawkes and Dorflinger popularized this star. The star center varied with the pattern (S 187). Some patterns crosshatched or added single stars to the spaces around points (S 188).

S 188. Crosshatched diamonds fill spaces around this 8-inch tall vase.

S 187. The 8-point stars circle the center on this 8-inch bowl.

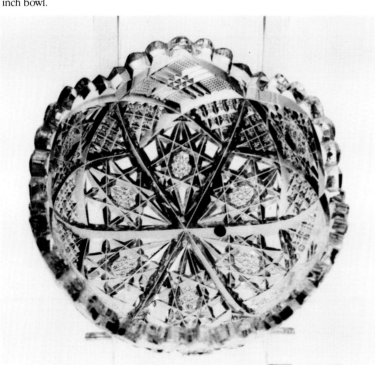

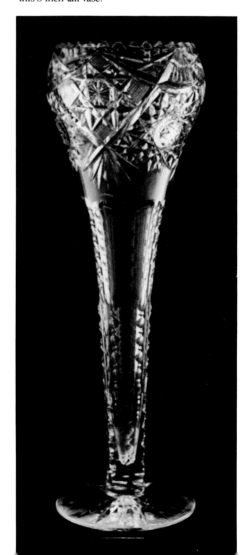

C 189. A 5-point star dominates this 14-inch flower holder signed Libbey.

C 191. A flat star alternates with a crosscut diamond in the cutting of this 6-inch, tall rose globe.

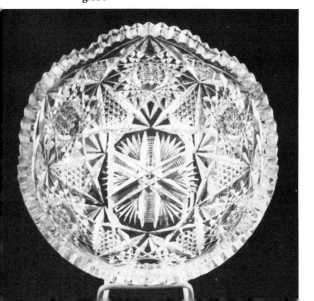

5-Point Star: Libbey introduced this star as a focal center or connecting motif in patterns (C 189).

Hobstar: The raised hob in the center gave this very popular star its name (P 190). Intersecting miters formed the points of the star and the facet center. The number of points, eight to sixty-four, depended on the pattern, the shape, the size, and the period cut. The raised center normally consisted of a single star within a small hobstar. With the rising costs of production later in the Brilliant Period, some companies used a flat star for the center. This flat star later became a dominant motif (C 191).

A few companies elongated the hobstar from top to bottom or from left to right (C 192). The most ornate of the hobstars formed small rosettes (P 193).

Flashed Star: Designers added fans between the hobstar points to produce this motif (C 194). A unique pattern by Tuthill flashed the tips of the hobstars (P 195).

P 190. A 32-point hobstar decorates this 8.5-inch, tall comport.

C 192. This 8-inch bowl features the elongated hobstar.

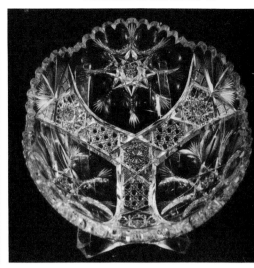

193. Rosettes alternate with hobstars on the 12-ch tray.

C 194. A 9-inch bowl with flashed stars.

C 195. On a 9-inch bowl Tuthill added fans to the point tips.

. **Buzzsaw**

In a buzzsaw curved miters with alternating fans gave the illusion of a spinning aw. Companies developed three different versions of this design.

Pinwheel: This motif included the most curved miters and fans. A hobstar formed he center (C 196). In several patterns the cutter combined the pinwheel with the obstar (P 197).

C 196. The Odessa Pattern by Clark featured pinwheels on the 10-inch, tall punch bowl.

C 197. A 14-inch, tall, punch bowl combines hobstar and pinwheel as a dominant motif.

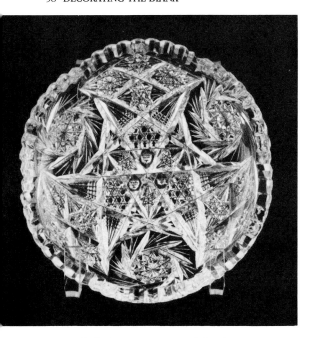

C 198. Buzzstars on a 9-inch bowl.

Buzzstar : The designer reduced the number of curved miters and fans for the buzzstar (C 198) but kept the hobstar center. Libbey simplified the center of the buzzstar (C 199).

Buzz: The buzz further reduced the number of miters, and, at times, used no fans at all (C 200). Today modern European glass patterns use the buzz.

4. Group Motifs

During the Brilliant Period of cut glass the designer combined a number of the same motifs to cover the entire blank or to serve a minor function. Such combined motifs filled small spaces in an ornate pattern.

Block: Perpendicular and parallel miters formed clear, flat-top squares. The blocks could cover the entire surface or serve as an individual motif (C 201). To make the block more decorative, companies placed an X on the clear space (C 202).

Pointed Diamond: In this motif curved miters intersected to form a tiny, sharp diamond (C 203).

Nailhead Diamond: The American craftsman removed the tip from the pointed diamond group to form the flat nailhead, (C204).

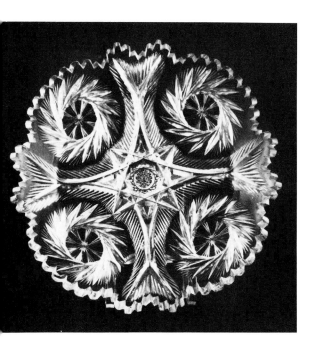

C 199. For the Sunset Pattern Libbey introduced a new center of turning fans.

C 200. A 13-inch vase with a buzz.

C 201. A 9.5-inch, tall cake tray with a block motif.

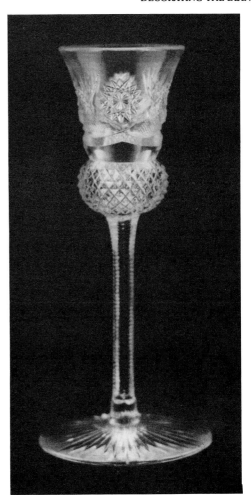

C 203. A cordial signed Libbey cut with the pointed diamond.

C 202. A 9-inch bowl with an X'ed block motif.

C 204. An 11-inch tray with nailhead diamond.

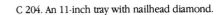

C 206. A 6-inch, tall rose globe with the crosscut diamond.

Cane: By enlarging the nailhead diamonds and separating them with intersecting miters, the designer created the group motif of cane (P 205).

Crosscut Diamond: Intersecting lines form a square upon which the craftsman cut a cross (C 206). As with the other groups, the motif formed a pattern, the Strawberry Diamond, or an individual motif.

Saint Louis Diamond: Originally this diamond consisted of concave circles that formed a border, an entire pattern, or decorative motifs on handles and necks of pieces. Later the Americans substituted a six-sided motif for the round one and called it "honeycomb" (P 207). Occasionally, you see it as the dominant motif on a vase (P 208) or bowl.

P 205. A 13-inch jug with a pointed oval of cane.

P 207. A 10-inch vase with honeycomb neck.

P 208. A 10-inch vase in Saint Louis Diamond Pattern.

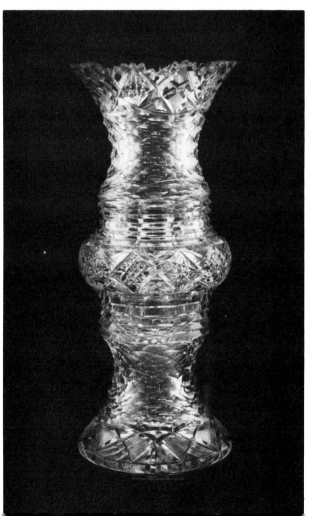

S 209. An 8-inch, tall comport with hobnails.

S 210. An 8-inch, tall carafe in Pattern #121 by Meriden notches the flutes on the neck.

Hobnail: This motif consisted of a round or hexagon button decorated with crosshatching. A number of companies cut a pattern of hobnails separated by intersecting miters and alternating with single stars (S 209).

Flutes: The group combined vertical panels with either a flat or a concave surface. Cutters often notched the edges for a decorative touch. Generally, designs called for flutes on the neck of a carafe (S 210), decanters, or oils, spouts of jugs, and on stems of heavy footed pieces.

These represent the basic, geometric motifs used in cut glass patterns. Constantly test your ability to recognize these motifs whenever you view a display of cut glass. In no time at all, you will recognize all of them and may discover others.

ENGRAVING

Engraving became popular midway in the Brilliant Period. Tuthill turned to intaglio while Sinclaire favored copper wheel engraving.

Intaglio

For intaglio, the craftsman pressed the blank against a stone wheel for cutting. This produced a sculpture effect, the opposite of cameo (P 211). The polisher purposefully left the design a silvery gray. Hawkes called his intaglio "gravic glass" and signed with a special signature. Both Libbey and Tuthill developed intaglio patterns.

P 211. A 7-inch, low bowl in Cosmos Star by Tuthill with flowers in intaglio.

212. An engraved, 9-inch bowl in Blackberry and Grapes Pattern by Tuthill.

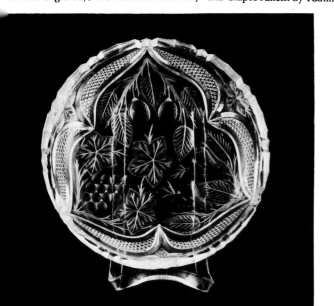

C 213. A clock signed Sinclaire in Adam 2 Pattern with copperwheel cut flowers.

C 214. A 9-inch comport with engraved print signed Sinclaire.

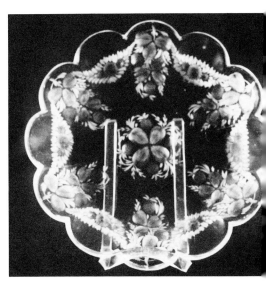

C 215. A 12-inch plate signed Libbey engraves clusters of nuts.

C 216. An engraved scene on a 7-inch plate signed Hawkes.

C 218. An 8-inch bowl with a decorated silver rim.

2. Copper Wheel

The wheel for this type of engraving varied in size from a pinhead to six inches. The craftsman worked with the copper wheel between him and the glass blank. The polisher purposefully left the design a silvery gray. Tuthill engraved fruit (C 212) and all types of flowers; Sinclaire seemed to prefer flowers (C 213) but also engraved fruit (C 214). For one pattern Libbey chose clusters of nuts (S 215). Hawkes signed a number of patterns depicting a scene (C 216) or a single object (C 217). Sinclaire may have created these before he organized his own company.

SILVER MOUNTINGS

No one can state when companies began to use silver mountings. In 1880, Mt. Washington Glass Works organized the Pairpoint Corporation to put silver on cut glass.

1. The Process

The glass company completely cut the pattern but left an uncut portion for silver fittings. The cutter leveled the uncut part of the item and sometimes cut notches in the glass to form a mechanical interlock (C 218). Then plaster of Paris held the silver to the glass.

The mountings consisted of sterling and plate. Silver plate adorn as much quality glass as sterling. When an item required a screw on top, the silver company contracted to do the work cut the groves to match the top. The width of the mounting depended on the size of the piece (P 219), but filigree ones needed more width (P 220).

Recently at an antiques show we saw a bowl signed Sinclaire with a silver deposit on the rim. A mixture of powdered chemicals, including silver, formed a solution the silversmith painted on a piece of glass and fired it to set the flux. Electroplating adheres the thin coat of silver to the piece.

C 217. A 4 by 5-inch dish with an engraved border and ship in Cristobel Pattern signed Hawkes.

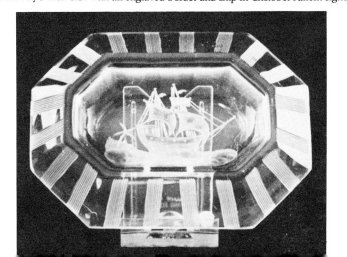

P 219. An ornate, silver rim on a 12 by 6-inch tray,
Gorham hallmark.

P 220. A 9-inch plate with a filigree, silver rim.

Mountings

A jewel box (C 221) needs silver for hinges. Silver went on bowls (C 222), ornate ollar (P 223) or plain one for a jug (C 224), or lids for a tobacco (C 225) or cracker r (D 226). Silver provided stoppers for decanters (C 227) and colognes (S 228). he candelabra consisted of silver with a glass base (P 229) as with this neck of a ower center (L 2 30). Bottles, such as bitter or pepper sauce, contained tops of lver. Look around you and you'll find other mountings of silver.

C 221. A 6-inch jewel box with silver hinged
fittings.

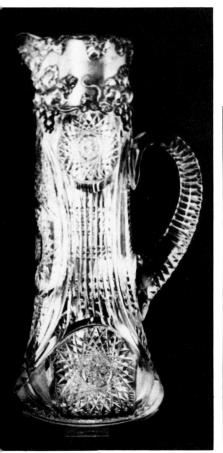

223. Ornate, silver collar on a 14-inch jug.

C 224. A plain, silver collar with Reed & Barton
hallmark on an 8-inch jug.

C 222. A 9-inch, divided bowl with a decorated
silver rim.

C 225. An 8.5-inch, tall tobacco jar with a silver lid.

C 226. A silver lid with handle on a six-inch, diameter cracker jar.

C 227. A decanter with a silver stopper.

S 228. A cologne with a silver stopper.

P 229. Pairpoint signed the silver on this candelabra.

L 230. Flower center in Gladys Pattern by Hawke and silver hallmark of Shreve.

COLOR CUT GLASS

Anyone owning a piece of American color-cut-to-clear glass has a true treasure for the cost curtailed extensive production. Research on patterns shows that Bergen, Clark, Dorflinger, Fry, Hawkes, Hoare, Libbey, Pairpoint, and Pitkin & Brooks produced this type of glass.

1. Production

Americans overlaid the color. The process used two pots of metal: a clear and a nearby one of the chosen color. The gatherer handed the blower a blob of clear metal to blow into a small bulb for the piece. The gatherer then dipped the enlarged bulb into the colored metal and rotated it until the color reached the desired thickness. Then the small bulb went back to the blower for completion of the shape. This overlay process always shows a division between the colored and the clear edge.

The lead content of the metal resulted in vibrant colors of green, ruby, amber, blue, amethyst, and rainbow. The shades of these colors varied from batch to batch: ruby to cranberry, amber to apricot, and green to aqua. At the end of the day most blowers filled the pipe with the remaining colored metals to blow rainbow.

2. Patterns and Shapes

Americans selected sparsely cut patterns so the color dominated. The Russian pattern, however, proved the exception. At first the patterns duplicated those of clear cut glass, but later the master craftsman created some original designs. Previously most patterns decorated sets, such as decanters and wines, carafes and tumblers, jugs and stemware. Original designs went on bowls, nappies, trays, or plates.

3. Identification

To identify colored glass, try to find a duplicate in the clear. Few companies signed the colored glass. Libbey signed some ruby wine glasses, Clark a fluted green punch cup, Hawkes a ruby decanter in Chrysanthemum, and Fry a cobalt blue carafe. Only Hawkes pictured colored glass in a catalog: two dinner bells, a claret, and a hock in ruby or green—these in Strawberry-Diamond and Fan and in Russian. For an educated guess, study the basic characteristics of the pattern and see if you can relate them to a company.

You now know how companies decorate blanks. Combine this knowledge with pattern outlines to give you the total picture for analysis.

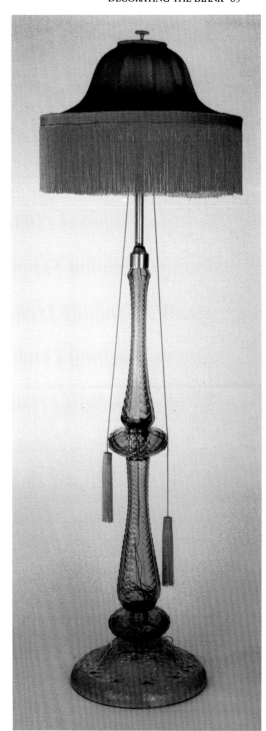

2. Hawkes gave Mr. Lightner this floor lamp in the Golden Flame Amber Pattern.

1. A cologne with a corded handle and tassel.

3. A wine bottle with oval panels of cane.

5. Dorflinger failed to name this pattern on a decanter but Pairpoint called it Cambridge.

4. Dorflinger cut this decanter with a handle and matching stopper in Heavy Flute Pattern.

6. A jug cut in a dual motif outline with matching stopper and a decorated handle.

8. The fitted, silver top of this decanter in Chrysanthemum by Hawkes has a thumb hold for pouring.

7. A Canadian rum jug with a music box that plays "How Dry I Am."

9. This decanter in Chrysanthemum by Hawkes has a silver, bird-like top.

10. An oval tray with a star miter outline.

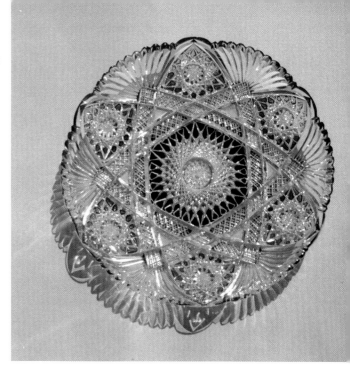

11. Hawkes cut this tray in the Savoy Pattern.

13. Cane decorates the points of the stars on this tray.

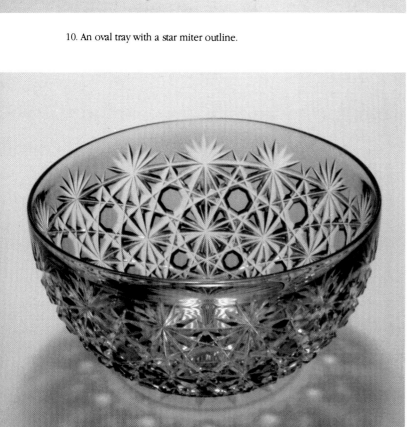

12. A bowl in Russian. Lightner Museum.

14. A tall comport in a rare blue-cut-to-clear design.

15. A plate in a Strawberry-Diamond and Fan Pattern.

16. A celery with a star as the miter outline.

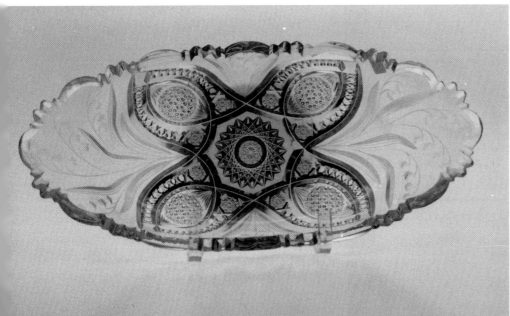

17. A tray in the experimental glass cut by Empire.

18. An individual salt.

19. A Plate in Parisian by Dorflinger.

20. The pattern on this bowl combines the featured bar with the buzzstar as the dominant motif.

21. Hobstars dominant this bowl in a dual motif outline.

22. A lidded jar in a pattern of punty border and crosscut diamonds.

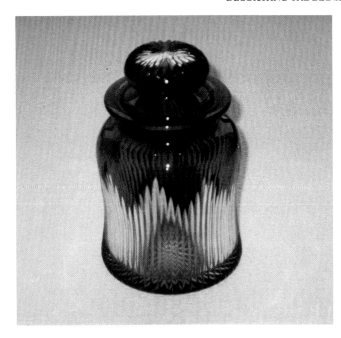

23. A cracker jar in Renaissance by Higgins & Seiter.

24. This rose globe in Croesus Pattern has straight miters rather than curved but signed Hoare.

25. A ringtree, rare because companies did not produce many, especially in color.

27. A bowl cut with the dual motif outline of cane and hobstar.

26. A saucer in an unusual apricot color and pinwheel motif.

28. A plate cut with a distinctive star outline.

29. An unidentified bowl.

30. A rare cup and saucer in a Russian Pattern.

31. A whiskey tumbler with an applied handle.

32. A cup and saucer in Plain Flute Pattern by
Libbey.

33. A tubular vase with rows of hobstars.

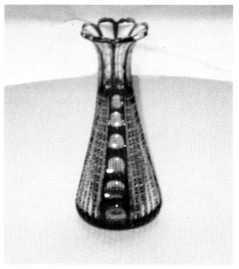

35. A vase in Boston Pattern by Pairpoint.

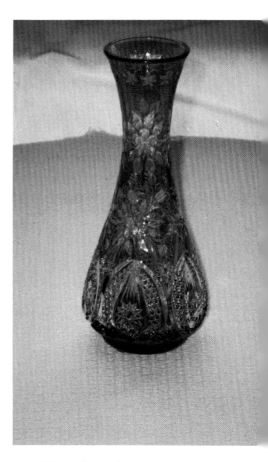

36. A vase that combines engraving with geometric cutting.

34. A solid color vase Pitkin & Brooks signed under the base.

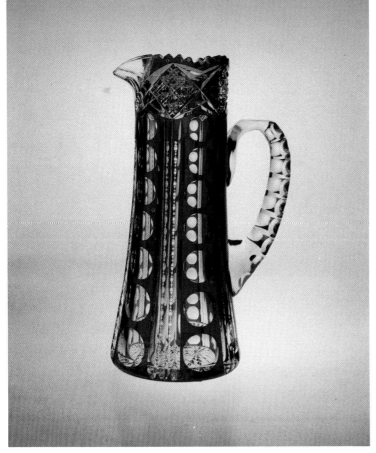

37. A wine jug in Henrietta Pattern by Pairpoint.

38. Mt. Washington produced this jug in the Split Punty Pattern.

39. A jug in Penrose Pattern by Hawkes.

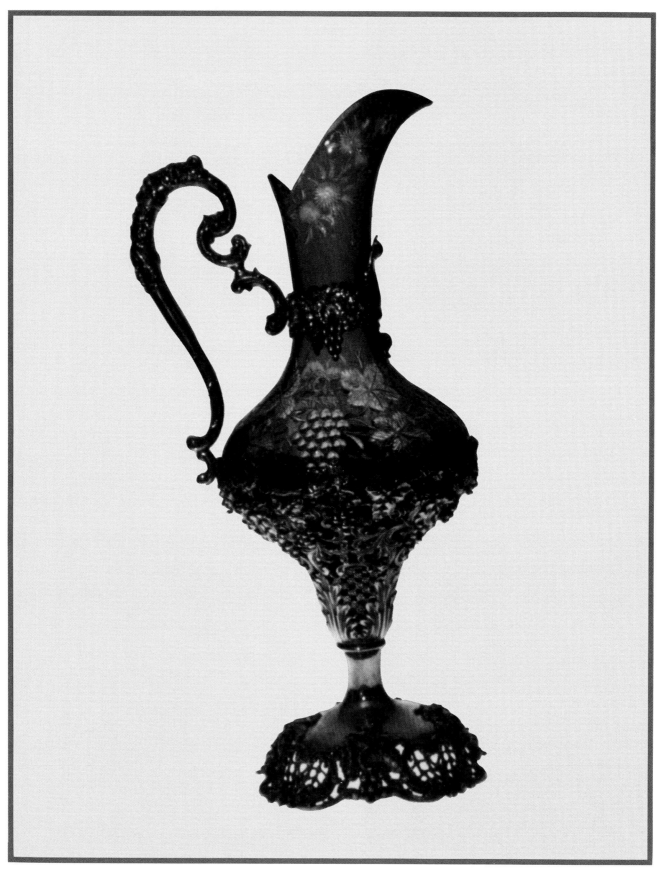

40. The silver holder enhances the ewer in
Viscaria Pattern by Pairpoint.

41. A silver topped jug in a bar outline with hobstars as dominant motifs.

42. A lemonade jug with a hobstar as a dominant motif.

44. A wine jug with a silver mounting.

43. A silver rim on a jug in Marlboro with engraving on the neck produced by Dorflinger.

45. A claret with hobstars as the dominant motifs.

46. A claret cut in rows of punties and of diamonds.

47. A claret in a dual motif outline.

48. A claret cut in an unnamed Dorflinger pattern.

49. Spreading fans form the border for the cane cutting on this claret.

50. A claret in Monarch by Hoare.

51. A vase in pattern #83 by Libbey.

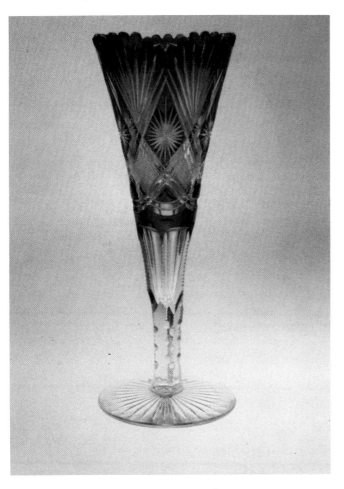

52. Higgins & Seiter shows this vase in a catalog as Evert Pattern.

53. Dorflinger did not give a name or number to this pattern or a vase.

55. Dorflinger cut this claret in Strawberry Diamond Pattern.

54. A claret with a punty border for a Strawberry Diamond pattern and with a notched stem.

56. Averbeck named this pattern on a Rhine wine Florida.

57. A Rhine wine with a heavily decorated stem.

58. A Rhine wine with double rings on the stem.

Chapter 5
Pattern Outlines

The dazzling beauty of cut glass denies any suggestion of a formal pattern. Yet a closer examination of any piece will reveal a basic outline for a pattern. When the master craftsman created a geometric pattern, he first outlined the design on the blank with miters. Then he filled in the motifs (C 231). The rougher took a model or sketch of a pattern and cut the miter outline before giving the piece to the smoother to fill in the motifs. The less talented roughers drew the miter outline on the blank with a grease pencil before cutting. This assembly-line approach to cutting made each craftsman a specialist. In smaller companies, however, one man did all these function. Consequently a pattern consists of two parts: the miter outline and the decorative motifs (P 232).

THE MITER OUTLINES

To match the miter outline of a pattern to pictures for identification mentally eliminate the motifs. This requires constant practice and concentration at first, but you soon learn to separate the miter outline from the motifs. Once you discover the miter outline, look only at pictures that duplicate it. This shortens the matching time. The type of miter outline can suggest the probable company, the date of cutting, and the quality of the piece. Knowing the ten types of miter outlines can simplify your search.

. Bars

In this miter outline bars dominated the pattern. The actual arrangement depended somewhat on the shape of the piece. In a standard design intersecting bars formed a cross that may or may not extend to the rim (S 233) or shaped a

C 231. Miters outline a simple pattern on an 8-inch bowl.

P 232. An oval, fruit bowl with a miter outline in Wheat Pattern by Hoare.

S 233. A 7-inch, divided nappy with two handles in Jupiter Pattern by Meriden. The bars form a cross.

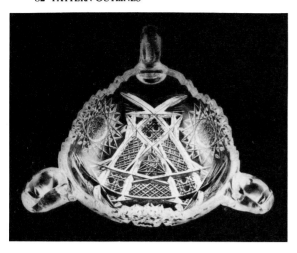

S 234. Bars form a triangle on this 5-inch, 3-handled nappy.

S 235. A 7-inch, oval bonbon where intersecting bars form a square.

C 236. On a cereal jug, 5-inches tall, vertical bars cross intersecting ones that frame hobstars.

triangle in the center (S 234). In another piece four bars intersected to create a square (S 235), or several diagonal ones framed hobstars separated by a vertical bar (C 236). Jugs used a circular bar (C 237) or diagonal ones to form a square (C 238).

The width of the bar, a half to two inches, varied with the size and the pattern. All craftsmen decorated the bars: steps (C 239), crosscut diamond (S 240), or alternated hobnails and stars (C 241). While most patterns used parallel lines to form the bar, more ornate patterns curved the bars (C 242).

C 237. Circular bars cross vertical ones on a jug 14-inches tall.

C 238. On a footed jug, 9.25-inches tall, diagonal bars frame hobstars.

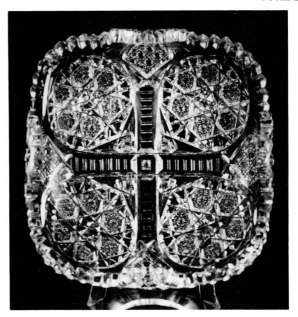

C 239. Steps decorate the bars in this 8-inch, square bowl.

C 240. On this leaf bonbon crosscut diamonds cover the bars.

C 241. Stars alternate with hobnails to decorate the bars of this 12-inch fruit bowl.

C 242. Curved bars outline the pattern on this 11-inch, square dish.

C 243. Repetitive motifs fill the rows on this 9.5-inch jug.

C 244. An 11-inch plate has equal spacing for the motifs.

2. Rows

Intersecting miters formed rows that framed repetitive motifs (C 243). The miters usually provided equal spacing for the motifs (C 244), or in some rounded shapes made the spacing in the top row larger than the lower one (P 245). With a round tray the spacing remained the same (P 246).

P 245. Spacing for motifs on a 13-inch, low bowl (handles included) decreased proportionately as rows circled toward the center.

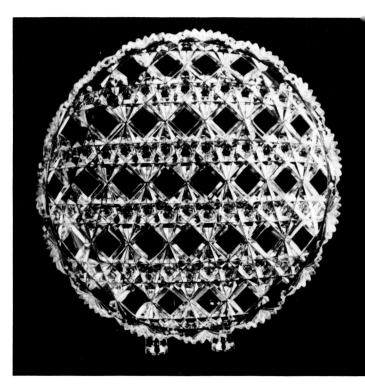

P 246. A 10-inch tray contains alternating rows of equal spacing.

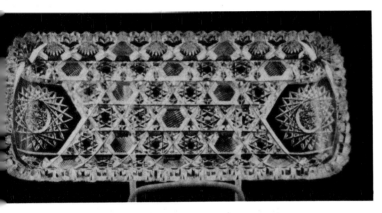

C 247. One or more repetitive motifs decorated the rows on this 12-inch tray.

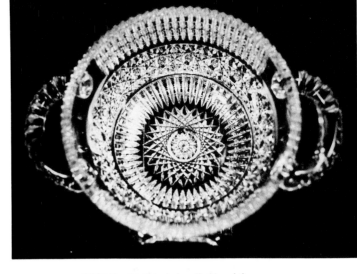

P 248. On this 9-inch, handled bowl the alternating rows used the same decorations.

The rows may provide spaces for one or more repetitive motifs (C 247). Frequently the shape contained two alternating rows with different motifs (P 248). One designer cut triple miters to frame the stars (C 249). For a decorative pattern the craftsman designed the rows in clusters to suggest a combination major motif (P 250). With most pieces of cut glass the row outline offered easy identification.

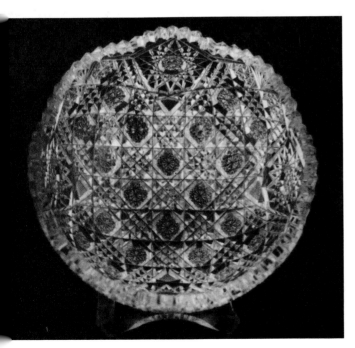

C 249. Triple miters bounded the rows in this 8-inch bowl.

P 250. A row outline on an oval fruit bowl, 9 inches in length, created an illusion of a cluster.

S 251. Tooth powder bottles, 5.5 inches tall, in Pattern #48 by Libbey used no border.

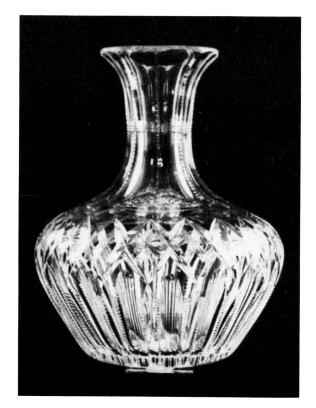

C 252. An 8-inch carafe added a border to the miter outline.

C 253. A vase, 13.5 inches, split the border of hobstars and crosshatching with notched miters.

3. Border and Miter

At first the master craftsman designed the pattern with notched miters and no border (S 251) and then made it more ornate with a border (C 252). The craftsman soon learned that a border added richness to a piece of cut glass (C 253).

The notching needed more elaboration to equal the border or else simplify the border (P 254). Some continued to make both the border and the miters ornate (P 255). The most ornate outline left spaces to alternate decorations on miters and border (C 256). For the Westminister Pattern Sinclaire (S 257) and for the Brunswick Pattern Hawkes used two borders (S 258).

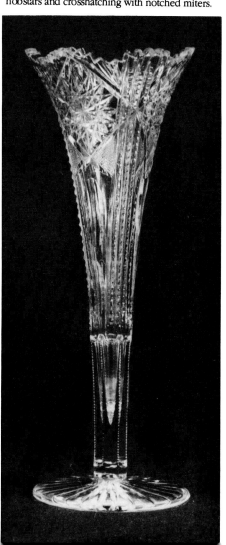

P 254. An 8-inch jug simplified the border but divided the notched miters with bars of triple cane.

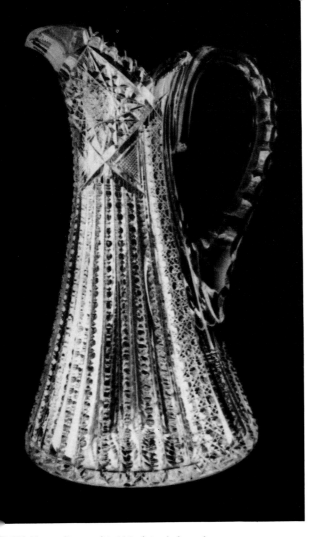

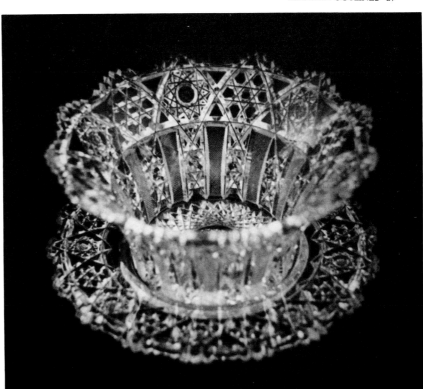

C 256. A 9-inch salad bowl imitated the border and miter outline but substituted other motifs for the notched miters.

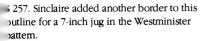

255. The outline on this 11-inch jug balanced the motifs of the border with the notched miters and cane bar.

S 258. A 6.5-inch, rose globe in Brunswick Pattern by Hawkes added another border.

257. Sinclaire added another border to this outline for a 7-inch jug in the Westminister pattern.

P 259. A 12-inch plate signed Libbey extended the points of the star to the rim.

C 260. The star on a 7-inch basket focused only on the center.

C 261. On this butter pat in the patented pattern #22662 Daniel Forbes cut only the star center.

C 262. The star outline joins the major motifs, the hobstars.

4. Star

The star outline varied with patterns and shapes. It formed a star from center to rim (P 259). The star may focus only on the center (C 260). On small pieces the craftsman may cut only the star center (C 261). It may join the major motifs (C 262).

The outline of the star to the rim could stretch the imagination. A six-point star placed the focus on four hobstar (P 263). A stretched outline supported four major and four minor motifs (C 264). Fans separated a pair of center points from three or either end (C 265) in one pattern. In an ornate pattern the miters overlaid three outlines for stars (C 266).

Decorations on and around the center star can almost hide it from detection (P 267). An elongated star joined the major motifs in one design (S 268). Some miter outlines of a star you may find quickly while others require a little search.

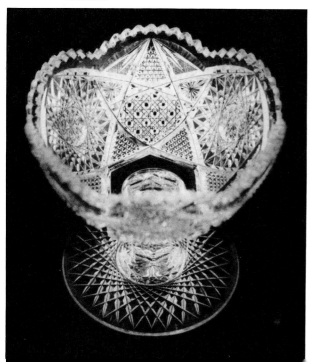

C 263. A tray, 12.5 by 8.5 inches, focused 4 of the 5 star points on hobstars.

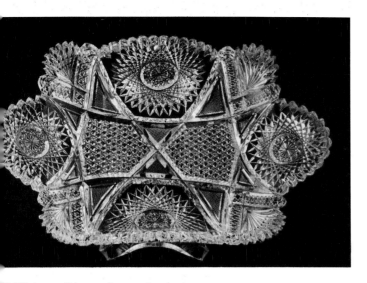

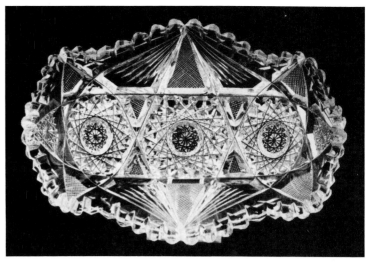

C 264. A tray, 13 by 8 inches, used a stretched, 8-point star to outline spaces for both major and minor motifs.

C 265. On a 10-inch bread tray, reverse fans in center separated two star points from the three at either end.

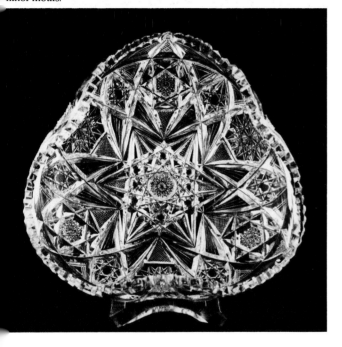

P 267. Heavy cutting on this 9-inch bowl almost hid the star center.

C 266. The miters on a 10-inch tray overlaid three star outlines.

S 268. In this mayonnaise, 6.5 by 4.5 inches, the star stretches to join the hobstars.

C 269. A 9-inch bowl in Chrysanthemum Pattern by Hawkes possibly inspired the gothic arch outline.

C 270. An 8-inch bowl with peg feet has single gothic arches.

5. Gothic Arch

The Gothic arch possibly developed from the Chrysanthemum Pattern (C 269) b Hawkes. Two pairs of curved miters intersected to form a pointed arch topped with star. The arch resembled the steeple of a Gothic church. The craftsman develop tw types of arches: single (C 270) and double (C 271).

In the single arch, double curved miters form the sides. Decorations on these sid lines include: notches (C 272), steps (P 273), or cane (P 274). In ornate patterns, th arches may lead to hobstars (P 275). A combination design may alternate betwee the arches (P 276). In one pattern the craftsman outlined arches grouped side b side (P 277). The center of the arch varied with the ornateness of the pattern.

The double gothic formed an upward and downward arch. The double arch ma alternate with a combination motif (C 278) or frame a dominant motif (P 279). Yo can readily locate either the single or double gothic arch in a pattern.

C 271. Double arches outline the pattern on this 7.5-inch relish.

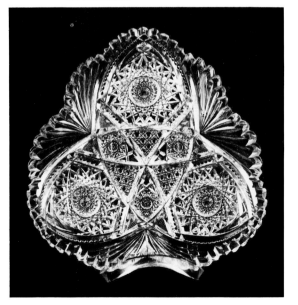

C 272. Notched miters outline the three arches on this 10-inch tray.

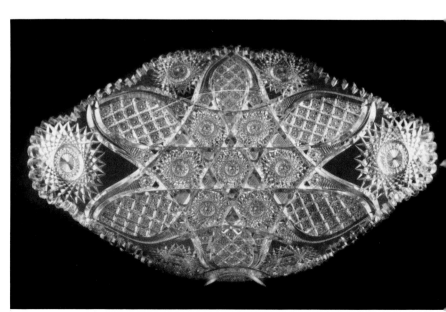

P 273. Steps decorated the arch outline on this 8 by 10-inch tray.

P 274. Cane covered the arch outline on this 12-inch decanter.

P 275. On a square dish, 8 inches, the double arches frame spaces for hobstars.

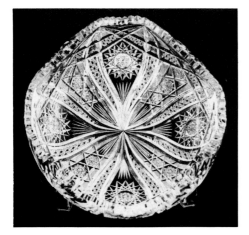

P 276. On an 8-inch, crimped bowl combination motifs alternated with the double arches around the hobstars.

P 277. A 9-inch, tall carafe with triple arches.

P 278. Double arches on a 7-inch plate alternated with a combination of motifs.

P 279. In a 12-inch decanter, the double arches frame the alternating, major motifs.

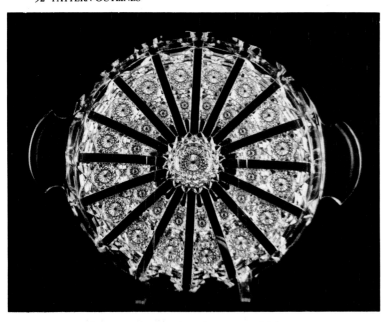

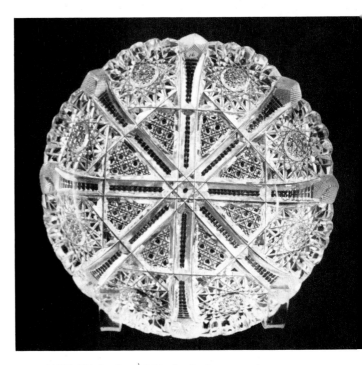

P 280. Clear miters outlined the panels of this 10-inch tray in Panel Pattern by Hawkes.

P 281. This low bowl, 8.5 inches in diameter and signed Straus, step cut the dividing miters.

6. Panels

Wide miters that radiated from the center to the rim formed the panels on a round piece. Hawkes left the dividing outline clear (P 280). A pattern by Straus step-cut the miters (P 281). In a heavier cut pattern Hawkes covered the miters with cane (P 282). Vertical miters divided the panels on a tall vase (P 283) or jug (P 284).

Decorations within the panels favored hobstars. Some panel patterns alternated the design (P 285) or feathered the panels (P 286). The globe of a lamp adapted well to panel outline (P 287).

P 283. Triple miters separated the panels on this 22-inch vase.

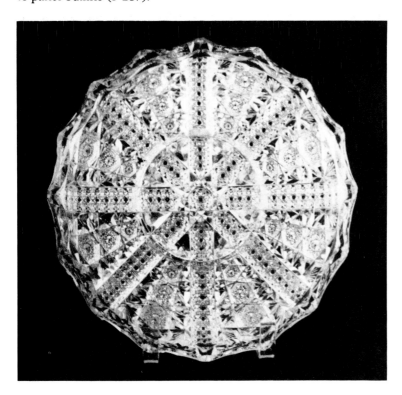

P 282. Cane decorated the miters in this 9-inch plate signed Hawkes.

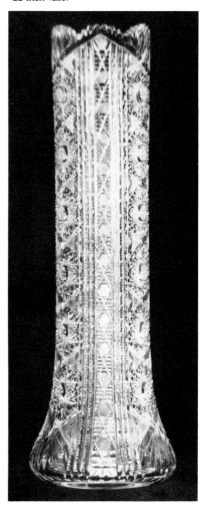

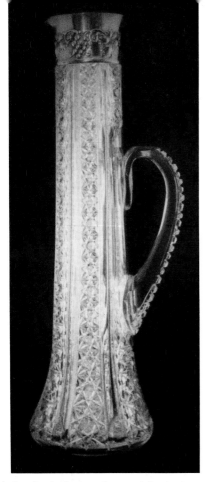

P 285. Clear miters separated the alternating panels on this 10-inch, low bowl.

P 284. Crosshatched miters decorated the dividers on this 18-inch jug.

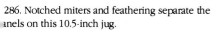

286. Notched miters and feathering separate the anels on this 10.5-inch jug.

P 287. Step-cut panels alternated with those of hobstars on this 20-inch lamp.

C 288. An 8-inch jug in Princess Pattern by Hawkes contained panels of punties and of six-point stars.

S 289. Whirling miters and stems led to a border of daisies on this 6-inch plate in a simple swirl outline.

P 291. A 9-inch bowl repeated the motifs in the swirls.

7. Swirls

When Edmund Halley predicted the appearance of a comet, he inspired a numbe[r] of companies to create such a design on cut glass. The fact that Halley's comet di[d] not appear until 1910 did not damper artistic endeaver earlier. Libbey and Hoa[re] possibly created the best know patterns in "comet", perhaps a descriptive nam[e]. The simplest type of comet swirled only in the center toward flowers on the bord[er] (S 289). A vase swirled the miters to a border (P 290).

The motifs in a swirl may repeat (P 291) or include several different ones (P 292). A miter outline may reverse the swirl (P 293). On occasion the swirl occupied th[e] lower part of a vase (P 294) or circled a wine decanter (P 295). The Laurel Cut Gla[ss] Company grouped miters of four to circle a hobstar border (C 296).

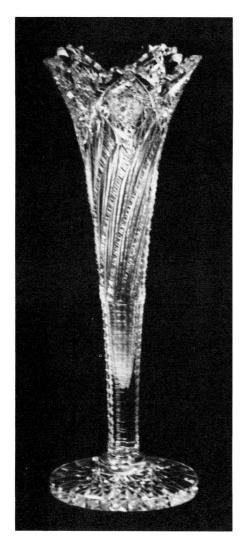

P 290. A 14-inch vase signed Hawkes spun notched miters to a hobstar border.

P 292. Three types of decorated swirls radiated from a pinwheel center on this 9-inch bowl.

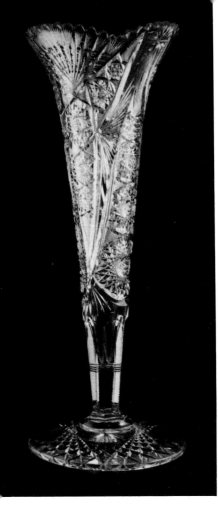

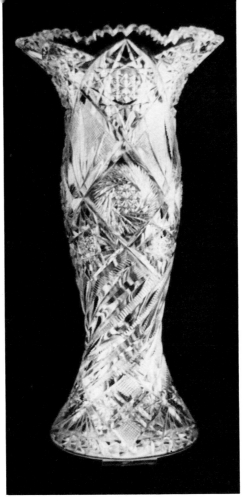

293. A 12-inch vase turned a swirl one way and then reversed the direction.

P 294. Only the lower part of a 12-inch vase contained a swirl outline.

P 295. A swirl circled this 10-inch decanter.

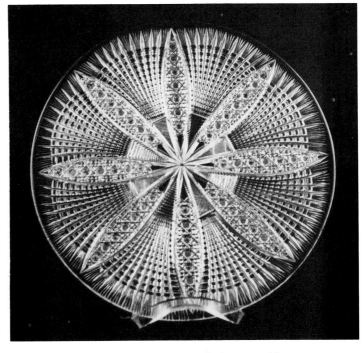

C 296. Feathered miters swirled from a pinwheel center to a hobstar border on this 8-inch bowl by Laurel Cut Glass Company in the Sylvia Pattern.

P 297. On a 12-inch plate pointed loops decorated with cane radiated from a focal center.

P 298. Pointed loops separated the hobstars in the 15 by 10.5-inch oval, fruit bowl.

C 299. In an 8-inch bowl pointed loops separated clusters of hobstars.

P 300. The miter outline provided border loops within the larger ones on this 7-inch bowl.

8. Pointed Loops

In this outline pointed loops radiated from the center (P 297) or created space for major motifs (P 298) or clusters (C 299). To provides for more motifs, the craftsman cut border loops within the large one (P 300) and then broadened them (P 301). Double loops within a loop separated the hobstars (C 302). The pointed loop outlined the very ornate patterns but recognizing them poses no problem.

P 301. This 5 by 6-inch bonbon contained two pairs of loops and a single one within a larger loop.

P 302. The pattern provided for three loops within a larger one on this 6-inch plate.

P 303. The outline on this 8-inch bowl framed the circles with double miters.

9. Circles

A miter outline, generally speaking, circled a dominant motif on a bowl (P 303) or one on a vase (P 304). The craftsman may circle the spot for the dominate motif (P 305) or leave only a round space for a hobstar (P 306). The outline at times may alternate the circle with space for another dominant motif (C 307). A combination of motifs may join the circled hobstar (C 308). The circle may outline the center as well as the major motif (C 309). The outline can emphasize half circles (C 310). The circles stand out so strongly in a miter outline, you see them almost at once.

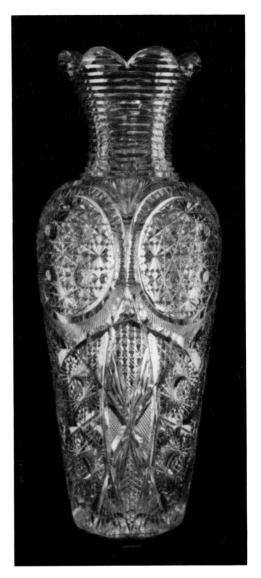

P 304. Step-cut miters included circles that formed part of the pattern on this 16-inch vase.

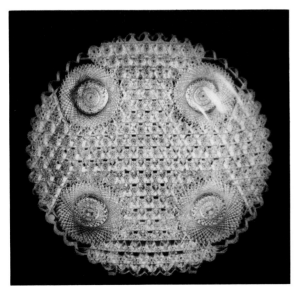

P 305. The miter outline left four round spaces in a group background for hobstars on this 12-inch tray.

P 306. In an 8-inch bowl, the outline left clear circles arranged in two rows for hobstars in a cane background.

C 307. The miter outline on an 8-inch, six-sided dish left circles on each side for hobstars.

C 308. An outline on a 9-inch, acorn tray left rounded spaces for the hobstars.

C 309. An 11-inch celery contained a double circle in the center and a single one on each side.

C 310. The miter outline created half circles for the pattern on this 11.5-tray.

S 311. A 6.5-inch plate contained a major (hobstar) and minor (elongated star) motifs in this geometric pattern.

C 312. The pattern on a flower holder, 11.5 inches, emphasized two major motifs: two flashed stars and a star combination of hobstars and flat ones.

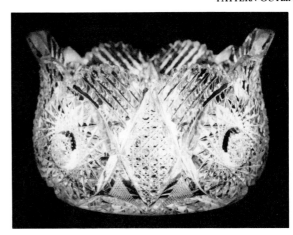

C 313. The outline for an ice tub, 6.5 by 4 inches, provided almost equal spacing for a major hobstar and alternate cane motif.

10. Dual Motifs

The miter outline can create spaces for four different types of motif arrangements, The pattern possibilities made this outline one of the most popular with both the large and small companies. The simplest pattern focused on a single major and minor motif (S 311). A number of patterns used two dominant motifs (C 312). In some patterns a minor group motif received the same importance as the dominant one (C 313).

A number of different patterns gave a combination of minor motif almost equal space with the major one (C 314). Another pattern reduced the size of the combination motifs and emphasized the dominant one (C 315). The size of the combination motif depended on the size and shape of the cut glass piece. The pattern outline enlarged the space for the combination motifs to compete with the major one (P 316) on large pieces. In smaller pieces the combination motifs often shared equally with the dominant one (S 317).

As you analyze the miter patterns, you'll see that some companies tended to repeat the same combination motifs in other patterns they cut. Some companies will favor the pinwheel while others the flashed star. Incidently, we have never found any record that shows Hawkes cut any patterns with buzzstars, but we keep looking.

C 315. A small combination motif linked the hobstars in the dual-miter outline of the 8-inch basket.

C 314. The pattern on this 12-inch decanter alternated between a hobstar and a combination motif.

P 316. Large pieces as this 13.5-inch, covered punch bowl required a more ornate combination design between hobstar.

S 317. The miter outline for this 6-inch vase equalized the size for dominant and combined motifs.

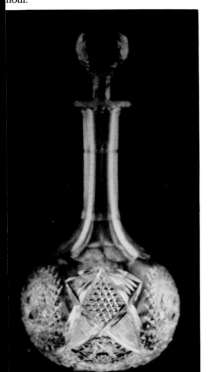

C 319. This 13-inch tray combined the bar and loop outline.

C 318. Bars and rows combined for the outline on this 9-inch bowl.

C 320. A combination bar and gothic arch pattern decorate this 14-inch jug.

11. Combinations

At the height of the Brilliant Period, the consumer wanted more and more ornate patterns. The master craftsman soon learned to combine two or more pattern outlines that accented the beauty of the glass.

Bars. The bar outline offered several combinations. Bars combined easily with rows (C 318) or as the inside of a loop (C 319). For large pieces bars united with the gothic arch (C 320) or with circles (C 321).

Star. A star outline combined artistically with circles (C 322) in one pattern outline and with gothic arch in another (P 323).

C 321 A pattern on a 14-inch jug consisted of bars and circles.

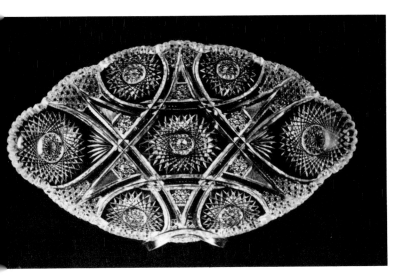

C 322. A tray, 17.5 by 10.5 inches, unites the star and circle outlines.

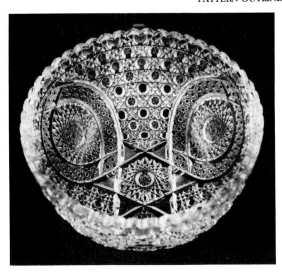

P 323. The star and gothic arch outlines formed the design on this 9-inch bowl.

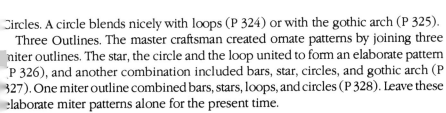

Circles. A circle blends nicely with loops (P 324) or with the gothic arch (P 325).

Three Outlines. The master craftsman created ornate patterns by joining three miter outlines. The star, the circle and the loop united to form an elaborate pattern (P 326), and another combination included bars, star, circles, and gothic arch (P 327). One miter outline combined bars, stars, loops, and circles (P 328). Leave these elaborate miter patterns alone for the present time.

P 324. Pointed loops and circles outlined the pattern on a tray, 13.75 by 8.5 inches.

P 325. A 14-inch jug overlaid the circle on the gothic arch to create the design.

P 326. Circle, pointed loop, and star outlines produced a heavily cut, 10-inch punch bowl.

P 327. A 10-inch punch bowl united bars, stars, gothic arches, and circles to form this pattern outline.

For now, concentrate on the ten basic outlines for patterns. In fact, you may want to re-read this chapter and study each illustration along with the text to develop a mental picture. By all means constantly test yourself each time you see a display of cut glass. Very soon you will know the excitement that goes with recognizing the miter outlines of basic patterns.

Even though you cannot find the pattern name or the company that produced it, you identify the piece of cut glass by miter outline. Possibly the outline might even lead you to the company that produced the piece. So let's use miter outlines in identifying patterns by individual companies.

C 328. An ornate outline on a 12-inch celery included bars, stars, and circles.

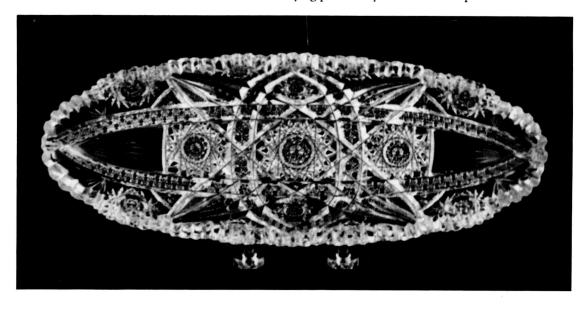

Chapter 6

New Identifications of Major Company Patterns

As a beginning collector you learned to identify public domain patterns cut by most companies, such as Strawberry-Diamond and Fan or Russian. When you became a more advanced collector, you could recognize popular patterns, such as Chrysanthemum by Hawkes or Alhambra by Meriden. As an advance collector you concentrate on identifying the patterns in your collection or those you plan to buy with an authentic source.

The verification of the following new patterns and those throughout this entire book developed from a study of old catalogs, published books and articles, old magazine advertisements, and patent records. To our knowledge the following identifications represent the first based on actual pieces of cut glass.

Remember, to identify a pattern on a piece of cut glass to a picture, first match the miter outline and then compare the choice and arrangement of the motifs. After you have used this method of identification for a while, you will recognize similarities repeated in different patterns by individual companies. Recognizing these similarities in other pieces you purchase can suggest a key to company identification. By listing the identifications by miter outline will take the first step for you in the matching process.

J. D. BERGEN COMPANY Meriden, Connecticut 1880-1922

Before James D. Bergen opened his own cutting shop, he worked for Mount Washington Glass Works, New England Glass Company, and Meriden Flint Glass Company. His patterns show a strong miter outline and extensive use of three or more motifs. He favored large pieces (P 329) and sets of jugs with tumblers or of decanters with wines.

1. GEOMETRICS
   Rows: Hibe (C 330), India (C 331)
   Border and Miter: Caprice (C 332), Penn (S 333), Prism (C 334)
   Gothic Arch: Bliss (P 335), Henry (P 336), plate patented July 5, 1892 (P 337)
   Pointed Loops: 6-inch plate Patent #27457 (C 338)
   Circles: Frisco (P 339), Niagara (C 340), Savoy (P 341)
   Dual Motifs: Delta (S 342), Dora (P 343), Elm (S 344), Sheldon (P 345), Star (S 346), Wallace (C 347)
2. FLORAL AND FRUIT
   Alpha (S 348), Berry (C 349), Clematis (C 350), Thistle (C 351), Rosebud with border (C 352), Rosebud (C 353)

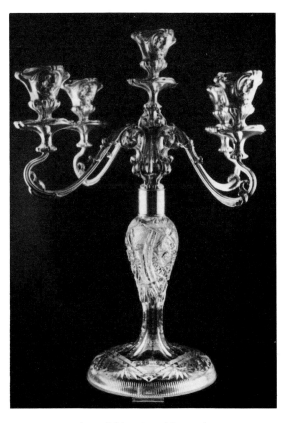

P 329. An 18-inch candelabra signed Bergen but shown in Pairpoint catalog as #6.

C 331. A 20-inch lamp in India by Bergen.

C 330. Bergen named this row pattern on a 9-inch plate Hibe.

C 332. A celery, 11 inches, in Caprice by Bergen.

S 333. A bonbon in Penn by Bergen.

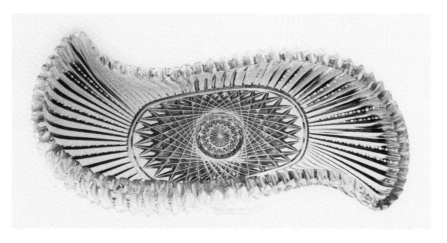

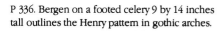

C 334. An 11-inch celery in Prism by Bergen.

P 335. Gothic arches outline the pattern on this 9-inch bowl in Bliss by Bergen.

P 336. Bergen on a footed celery 9 by 14 inches tall outlines the Henry pattern in gothic arches.

P 337. Bergen patented this pattern with gothic arches on July 5, 1892.

C 338. Bergen received patent #27457 for this pointed loops outline on a 6-inch plate.

P 339. A tray, 17.5 by 10.25 inches, in Frisco by Bergen.

C 340. Circles ouline this 5 by 6-inch bonbon in Niagara by Bergen.

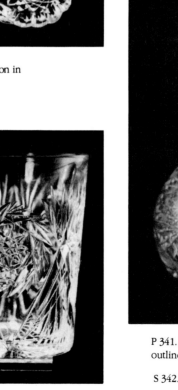

P 341. Bergen named this pattern in a circle outline on a 15-inch decanter Savoy.

S 342. Two tumblers in Delta by Bergen.

P 343. A one-piece, 10-inch punch bowl in Dora by Bergen with a combination and major motif.

S 344. A 4.5-inch saucer in Elm by Bergen.

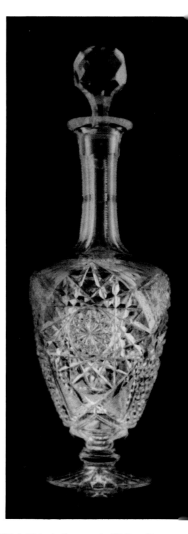

P 345. A 12-inch vase in Sheldon Pattern by Bergen.

S 346. A mustard in Star Pattern by Bergen.

C 347. A 12-inch decanter in Wallace Pattern Bergen.

S 348. Daisies dominate the Alpha Pattern in this 22-inch lamp signed Bergen.

C 350. A 10.5-inch comport in Clemantis Pattern by Bergen.

C 352. An oil in Rosebud Pattern by Bergen has a hobnail border.

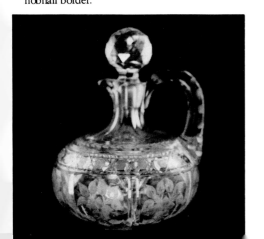

C 349. The Berry Pattern by Bergen on this 8.5-inch plate.

C 351. A two-part punch bowl in Thistle Pattern by Bergen.

C 353. The clock in Rosebud by Bergen has no hobnail border.

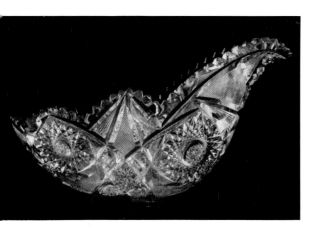

P 354. An odd shaped bowl, 8 inches, in Turquoise by Clark.

T. B. CLARK AND COMPANY, Honesdale, Pennsylvania 1884-1930

Thomas Byron Clark worked for the Meriden Flint Glass Company before establishing his cutting shop. Odd shapes, such as an oval bowl (P 354) and bonbon (C 355), intrigued him. Clark dared to leave the center of a hobstar blank (P 356) and showed a sense of humor when he called one butter pat Guernsey and the other Jersey (C 357)

1. GEOMETRICS

Bars: Azom (C 358), Cameron (C 359), Clairone (C 360), Coronet (S 361), Del Norte (S 362), Diana (C 363), Drexel (C 364), Genoa (P 365), Roxbury (C 366) Yuma (C 367)

Rows: Hollow Diamond (C 368)

Gothic Arch: Grecian (P 369)

Dual Motifs: A E (C 370), Creston (S 371), Grayling (C 372), Irvona (C 373), King (S 374), Lenox (S 375), Moonbeam (C 376), Nita (C 377), Olga (S 378), San Marco (S 379), San Mateo (S 380), Vanity (C 381), Violet (S 382), Virginia (S 383), Yoland (C 384)

Combination: Manhattan (S 385), El Paso (C 386), Holland (C 387)

Floral: flower center and geometric border.

C 355. A triangular bonbon in Myrtle Pattern by Clark.

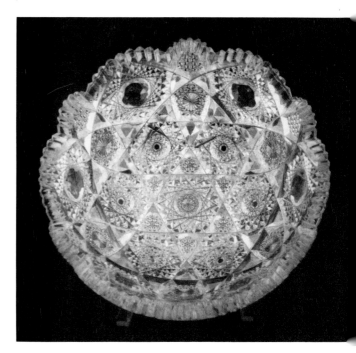

P 356. The hobstars have a clear center in a 10-inch bowl named Rembrandt by Clark.

C 357. Butter pats by Clark in Guernsey and Jersey patterns.

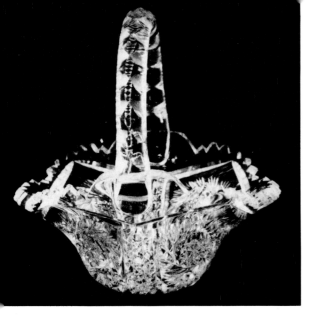

C 358. A 6.5-inch basket in Azorn by Clark

C 359. Bars separate the major motifs in Cameron Pattern by Clark.

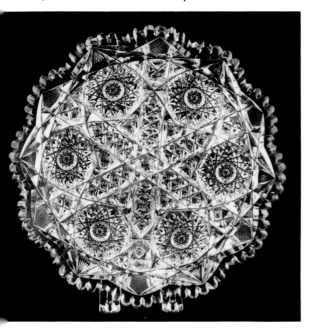

C 360. In Clairone Pattern by Clark, decorated bars separate the hobstars on this 10-inch plate.

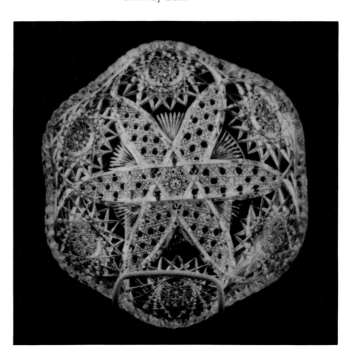

S 361. A 9-inch, crimped bowl in Coronet Pattern by Clark covered the bars with cane.

S 362. A single bar dominated this 7-inch relish in Del Norte Pattern by Clark.

C 363. Bars form a square in the Diana Pattern by Clark.

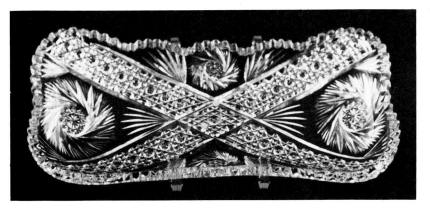

C 364. Intersecting bars dominate this 13-inch, bread tray in Drexel Pattern signed Clark.

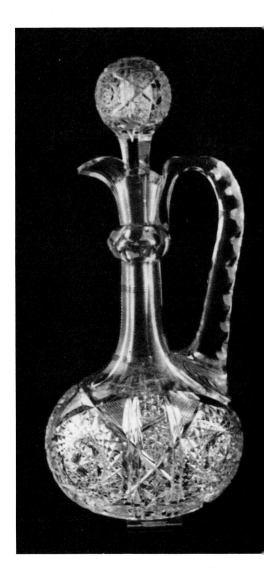

P 365. Hobstar decorate the bars in this handled decanter, 10-inches, in Genoa Pattern signed Clark.

C 366. On a 12-inch plate bars with flat stars separate the hobstars in the Roxbury Pattern signed Clark.

C 367. A double-handled, upright spoon holder with crosshatched bars in Yuma Pattern signed Clark.

C 368. An 8-inch candlestick in a row outline called Hollow Diamond Pattern by Clark.

P 369. Gothic arches outline the Grecian Pattern of this 9-inch bowl by Clark.

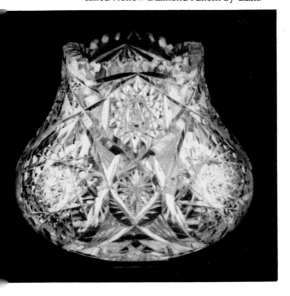

C 370. A 6-inch, rose vase in AU by Clark.

S 371. Clark named this pattern on a 7-inch plate Creston, cut in dual motifs.

C 372. A 10-inch comport in Grayling Pattern alternated between flat and flashed stars, with Clark signature.

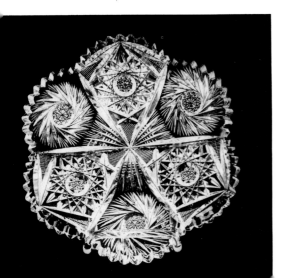

C 373. Clark called this 10-inch comport with dual motifs Irvona.

S 374. Wines in King Pattern and signed Clark.

S 375. A 6-inch bonbon with miters separating the hobstars in Lenox Pattern by Clark.

C 376. Clark signed this 6-inch tall comport in Moonbeam Pattern, cut with a shooting star.

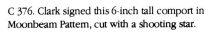

C 377. An 11-inch jug in Nita by Clark.

S 378. A tumbler in Olga by Clark with notched miters separating the hobstars.

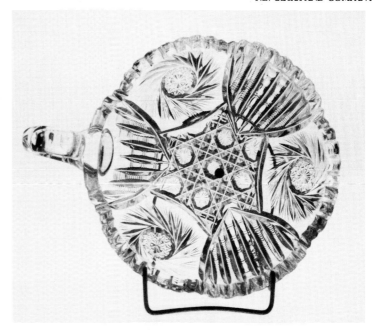

S 379. Clark signed this 6-inch nappy in the San Marcos Pattern featuring pinwheels.

S 380. A wine in San Mateo signed Clark.

S 382. A violet globe in Violet Pattern with single stars by Clark.

C 381. A 4 by 3-inch flower center in Vanity Pattern by Clark.

S 383. An 8-inch plate in Virginia by Clark.

C 384. A goblet with flat stars as major motifs in Yolanda Pattern signed Clark.

S 385. A 7-inch bowl in the Manhattan Pattern combined the row and star outline.

C 386. In the Holland Pattern Clark combined gothic arch and pointed loops on this 8-inch plate.

C 387. The El Paso Pattern by Clark united bars and circles.

C 388. Clark signed this 10-inch plate in a pattern of hobnail border and floral center.

C. DORFLINGER & SONS, Brooklyn 1852-1865
White Mills, Pennsylvania 1869-1921

Christian Dorflinger apprenticed at the St. Louis Glass Works in France where he learned the simple row patterns he cut at his factory in the United States. In later years he produced an exceptional line of both clear and colored cut glass. A shrewd business man, he sold both clear and colored blanks to cutting shops.

GEOMETRICS
Bars: Windsor (P 389)
Rows: Block Diamond (C 390), Colonial (S 391), Hob Diamond & Lace (C 392), Hollow Diamond or Honeycomb (C 393), Oriental (C 394), Star and Diamond (P 395), Willow (C 396)
Border and Miter: Clementis (P 397)
Star: Marathon (S 398)
Gothic Arch: Paola (C 399)
Pointed Loops: Alameda (C 400), Monclova (P 401)
Circles: Holland (p 402)
Dual Motifs: Lorraine (S 403), Savoy (P 404), Wimborne (C 405)
NUMBERED PATTERNS
Bars: #50 (P 406)
Rows: #1210 (P 407)
Dual Motifs: #18 (C 408), #20 (S 409), #293 (C 410), #350 (C 411),
UNNAMED PATTERNS
Border and Miter: basket (C 412)
Combination: nappy in bars and pointed loops (C 413)
FLORAL
Athens (S 414)
#1170 (S 415)
#175 (S 416)

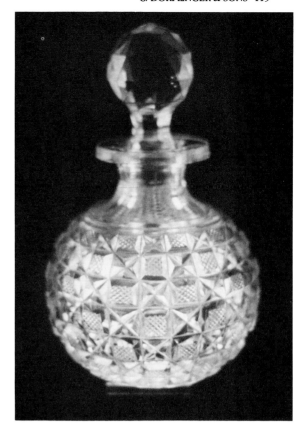

C 390. A cologne in Block Diamond Pattern by Dorflinger.

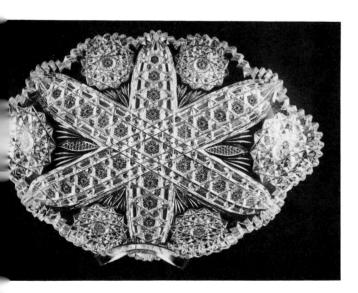

389. In this 15 by 10-inch tray, Windsor Pattern Dorflinger, bars dominate.

S 391. A 6.5-inch bowl in Colonial by Dorflinger.

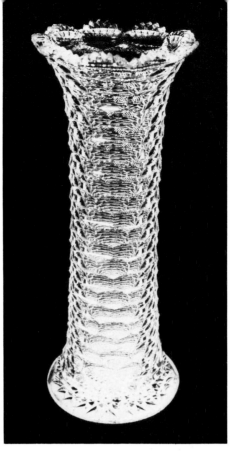

C 392. A 9-inch demijohn with lock in Dorflinger's Hob Diamond and Lace Pattern.

C 393. A row pattern by Doflinger, a 15.5-inch vase in Hollow Diamond or Honeycomb.

C 394. A 6-inch, upright spoonholder in Oriental by Dorflinger.

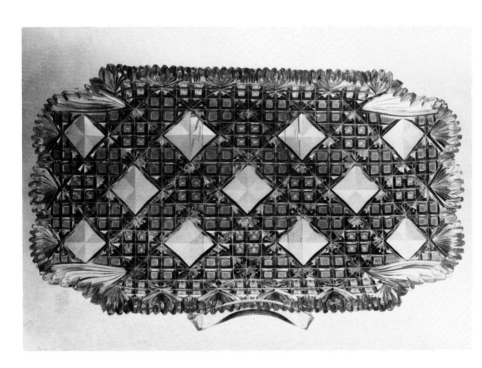

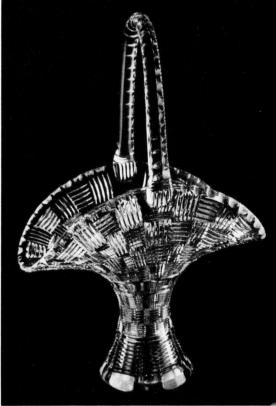

P 395. A row outline on a 15-inch tray in Star and Diamond Pattern. by Doflinger.

C 396. A basket in Willow Pattern by Dorflinger alternated vertical and hortizonal squares of miters.

P 397. A 7-inch, tall tobacco jar in Clementis Pattern by Dorflinger uses a border and miter outline.

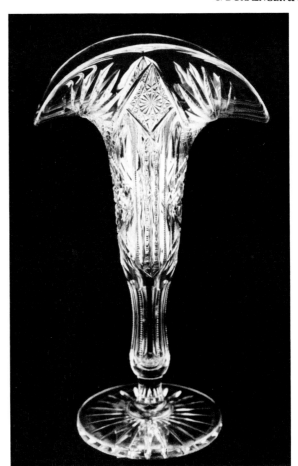

C 400. A 10-inch vase in Alameda Pattern by Dorflinger with a panel outline.

S 398. A star outline on a 6-inch plate in Marathon Pattern by Dorflinger.

C 399. A gothic arch outlined the Paola Pattern on this 13-inch tray.

P 401. Pointed loops outline the Monclova Pattern by Dorflinger on this 9-inch bowl.

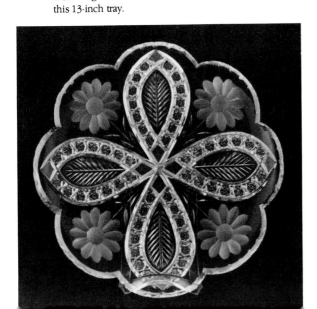

P 402. A 4.5-inch tall mushroom bowl and cover in Holland Pattern by Dorflinger used a circle outline.

S 403. A goblet, 6.5 inches tall, with dual motifs in Lorraine Pattern by Dorflinger.

P 404. A 9-inch, tall cigar jar in Savoy Pattern by Dorflinger with dual motifs.

C 405. The Wimborne Pattern by Dorflinger alternated motifs on this 12-inch tray.

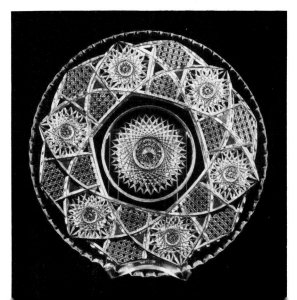

P 406. #50 identifies this bar pattern by Dorflinger.

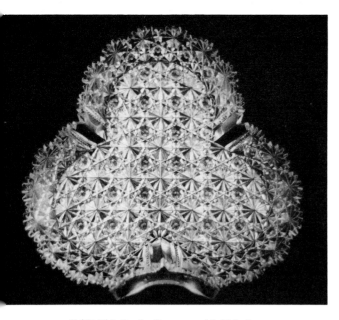

P 407. This Russian Pattern on this 12-inch tray Dorflinger numbered #1210.

C 408. A 10-inch tray Dorflinger gave the number #18.

S 409. A whiskey tumbler in #20 by Dorflinger.

C 410. A 10-inch bowl in #293 by Dorflinger.

C 411. A saucer, 5.5 inches, in Dorflinger's #350.

C 412. An unnamed pattern by Dorflinger used a Border and Miter outline for this 14-inch basket.

C 413. A 6-inch bonbon, identified as Dorflinger but unnamed, comblined gothic arch with pointed loops.

C 414. This 6-inch, tall comport has the flower of the Athens Pattern by Dorflinger but no border.

S 415. The daisy on this 6-inch nappy matches that on the Dorflinger Pattern #1170.

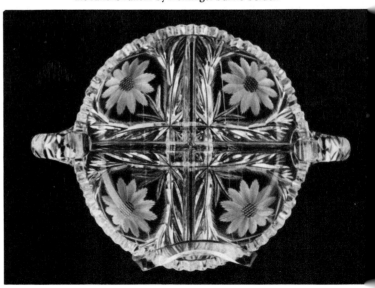

S 416. This doubled-handled nappy Dorflinger numbered #1175.

O. F. EGGINTON COMPANY, Corning, New York 1896-1918

Oliver Egginton came from a family long associated with the making of glass in England. When he immigrated to the United States, he became manager for Hawkes where his son, Walter, worked as a cutter. He later opened his cutting shop where his son and his daughter worked. "Papa was a true artist. He had the best acid bath. When he dipped the piece, he recited a nursery rhyme, then took it out of the acid." When asked which one, she looked surprised. "No one ever asked him."

Star: Genoa (P 417), Virginia (C 418)
Panels: Genoa #2 (P 419), Cambria (C 420)
Dual Motifs: Gloria (C 421)

P 417. A 7-inch jug in Genoa Pattern by Egginton with a star outline.

P 419. A vase. 10 by 3.5 inches, in a panel outline, Egginton identified as Genoa #2.

C 418. A 4.5-inch saucer in Virginia signed Egginton.

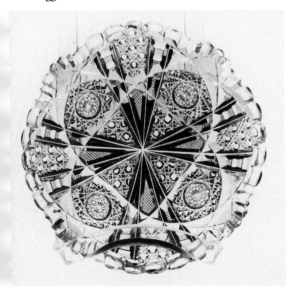

C 420. A 6-inch nappy in Cambria Pattern by Egginton in a panel outline.

C 421. Egginton named this pattern Gloria on this celery with dual motifs.

EMPIRE CUT GLASS COMPANY Flemington, New Jersey 1904-1923

H. C. Fry purchased this company and moved it to Flemington. Louis Iorio (L 42 and his son, Bill (L 423), created many of the company patterns. Fry and Empire of duplicate patterns. Fry used the company to experiment with a special type colored glass (See color section). At the beginning Empire used the fine lead blank produced by Fry, but in the last years it relied on the figured blank for floral piece

Bars: Argo (S 424), Elite (S 425)

Border and Miter: Peerless (S 426)

Star: Alex (S 427), Cambridge (S 428)

Swirl: Madeline (S 429)

Pointed Loops: Princeton (C 430)

Dual Motifs: Atlanta (S 431), Helena (S 432), Phillisburg (S 433), Rayner (C 43

L 422. An ash tray cut by Louis Iorio.

L 423. The late Bill Iorio at work.

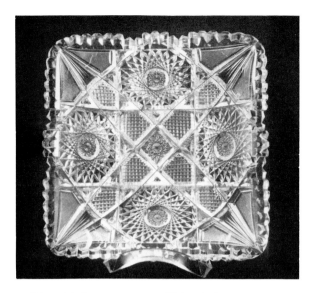

S 424. An 8-inch, square tray cut with bars in Argo Pattern by Empire.

C 425. The Elite Pattern by Empire cut with bars on an 8-inch, crimped bowl.

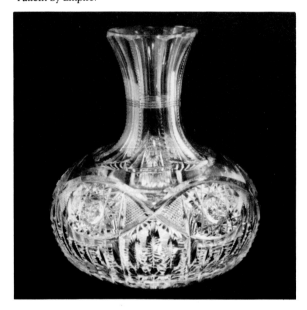

S 426. A carafe in Peerless by Empire used the border and miter outline.

S 428. A two-handled nappy in Cambridge by Empire has a star outline.

S 427. A 5-inch saucer in star outline pattern called Alex by Empire.

S 429. A puff box in Madeline Pattern by Empire in a swirl outline.

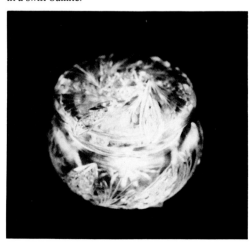

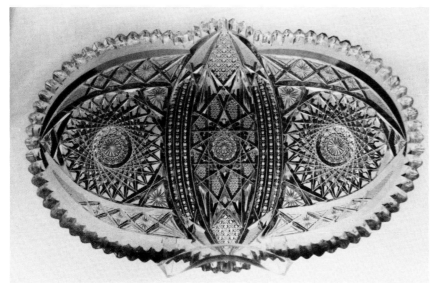

C 430. A 12-inch tray in pointed loops by Empire in the Princeton Pattern.

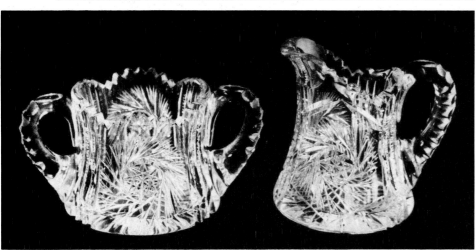

A 431. A medium sugar and cream in Atlanta Pattern by Empire used two motifs.

S 432. The Helena Pattern by Empire decorated this 12-inch plated with dual motifs.

S 433. A 9-inch bowl in Phillipsburg Pattern by Empire used the dual motif outline.

S 434. A 7-inch, tall comport in Rayner Pattern by Empire.

H. C. FRY GLASS COMPANY Rochester, Pennsylvania 1874-1934

Henry Clay Fry operated the Rochester Tumbler Company before he bought it and changed the name. He concentrated on making blanks with a high lead content that made cutting easier and more prismatic. As production cost rose, he used figured blanks but signed all, regardless of the type of blank. A grandson of the secretary of the company confimred that in the last years Fry etched a signature in block letters.

1. GEOMETRICS
   Bars: Star (C 435)
   Border and Miter: Meteor (S 436)
   Star: Zenith (C 437)
   Panels: American (C 438)
   Swirls: Sheraton (S 439)
   Pointed Loops: Esther (C 440)
   Circles: Washington (C 441)
   Dual Motifs: Alvin (S 442), Varden (S 443), Vienna (S 444), Zenda (S 445)
2. FLORAL AND FRUIT
   Daisy (C 446), Prism and Flutes (S 447), Raspberry (C 448)

C 435. In this 8-inch, tall carafe, bars separate the hobstars in the Star Pattern by Fry.

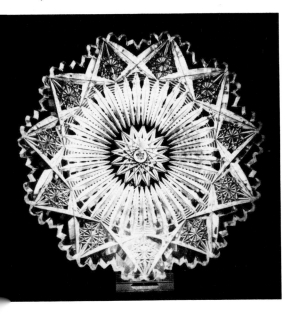

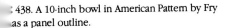

436. Fry's Meteor Pattern on this 7-inch plate sed a border and miter outline.

438. A 10-inch bowl in American Pattern by Fry as a panel outline.

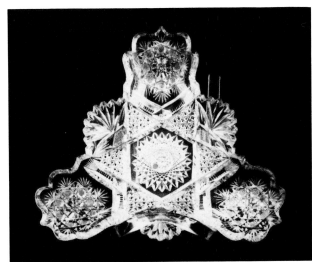

C 437. In the Zenith Pattern on this olive dish Fry cut a flashed star.

S 439. A 12-inch plate in Sheraton by Fry, engraving added a swirl.

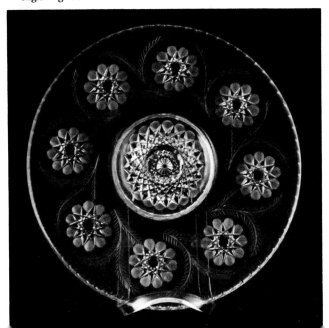

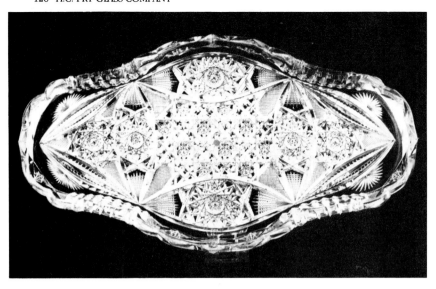

C 440. Pointed loops outlined the Esther Pattern by Fry on this dresser tray, 14.5 by 8 inches.

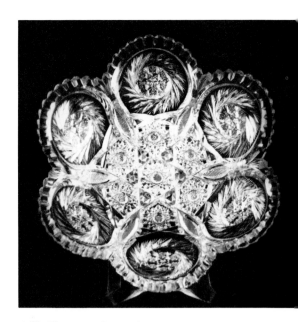

C 441. The crimped, 10-inch bowl accented the circle outline in the Washington Pattern by Fry.

S 442. Hobstars and fans formed the Alvin Pattern by Fry on this 11-inch celery.

S 443. An 8-inch vase signed Fry in Vardin Pattern.

S 444. A 4-inch, cereal jug in Vienna Pattern signed Fry.

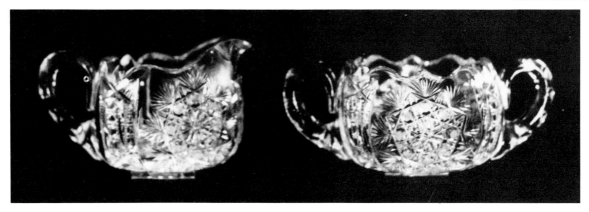

C 445. Fry signed this medium-sized sugar and
cream in Zenda Pattern with flashed stars.

446. A 12-inch tray with floral border and
ussian center Fry called Daisy Pattern.

C 448. A 6-inch plate in Raspberry Pattern signed
Fry.

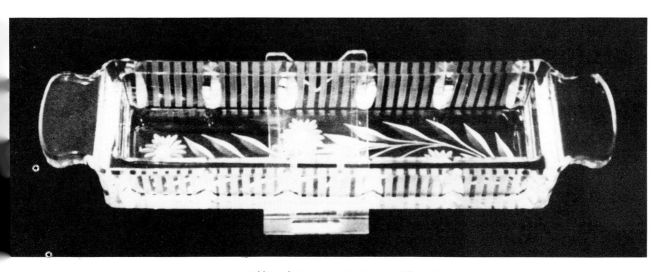

S 447. A domino sugar in Prism and Flutes Pattern
by Fry.

C 449. A 5-inch flower pot in Radiant by Hawkes.

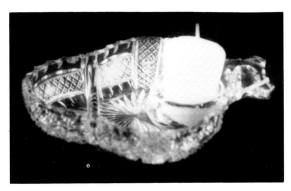

C 450. A candle holder in hortizonal and vertical bars of Strawberry Diamond by Hawkes.

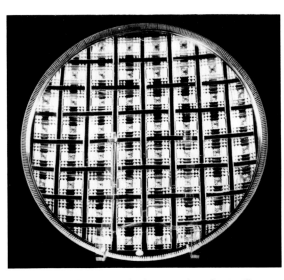

C 451. A 12-inch plate signed Hawkes in Albany, a row pattern.

T. G. HAWKES & COMPANY Corning, New York 1880-1962

Thomas Gibbon Hawkes came from a family associated with Waterford glass in Ireland. He received a degree in engineering before he immigrated to the United States. In this country he worked as manager for Hoare until he opened a cutting shop. His patterns show a simple exactness. He created a number of panel patterns that blended with the crimped shape. His large production rivaled that of Libbey.

1. GEOMETRICS

Bars: Radiant (C 449), Strawberry Diamond (C 450)

Rows: Albany (P 451), Alpine (C 452), Garnet (S 453), Jubilee (C 454), Old Irish (C 455), Palmyra (C 456), Pilgrim (C 457), Portland, (S 458), St. Regis (S 459) Strawberry Diamond (C 460), Victor (C 461)

Border and Miter: Cristobel (S 462), Isabelle (C 463), Newport Engraved (S 464) Strawberry (C 465)

Star: Pillars and Star (C 466)

Gothic Arch: Coronet (C 467), Savoy (C 468)

Panels: Colonial (S 469), Flutes (S 470), Lamont (S 471), Mona (S 472), Panel and Kohinoor (P 473), Panel and Punties (P 474), Tuetonic (C 475), Victoria (P 476) Winchester (C 477)

Swirls: Corn (C 478), Kohinoor (P 479)

Dual Motifs: Anson (C 480), Arcadia (S 481) Armanda (S 482), Brandon (C 483) Brighton (C 484) Brussels (P 485), Concord (S 486), Cypress (C 487), Dorthea (C 488), Florence (C 489), Harold (S 490), Kent (S 491), Mars (C 492), (C 493), Melrose (C 494), Mirage (C 495), Montrose (S 496), New Princess (C 497), Normandy (C 498), Odd (C 499), Odd (C 500), Premier (C 501), Pueblo (L 502), Raleigh (P 503) Tudor (C 504), Tyrone (S 505)

2. NUMBERED PATTERNS

Rows: #773 (S 506)

Star: #2 (S 507), #999 (P 508), #1417 (S 509)

Panels: #1 (S 510), #462 (P 511), #1189 (C 512), #1287 (P 513), #1302 (P 514) #1401 (P 515), #1407 (C 516), #1583 (C 517)

3. GRAVIC AND ENGRAVED

Floral: Gravic Carnation (C 518), China Aster (C 519), Chrysanthemum (S 520) Cosmos (S 521), Dahlia (C 522), satin gravic flower (S 523)

Fruit: Gravic Strawberry (C 524), Three Fruits (C 525)

Engraved: Empire (S 526), Josephine (S 527), Napoleon 1 (C 528)

4. SIGNED

Border and Miter: footed vase (S 529), tubular vase (C 530)

Star: nappy (S 531)

Pointed Loops: tray (P 532), club bonbon (C 533), heart bonbon (C 534 diamond bonbon (C 535)

Dual Motifs: oval fruit bowl (P 536), rose globe (C 537), footed vase (C 538 14-inch vase (C 539) decanter (P 540), tray (C 541), bowl (C 542)

Combinations: vase (C 543)

C 452. Hawkes named this pattern on an 8-inch bowl Alpine.

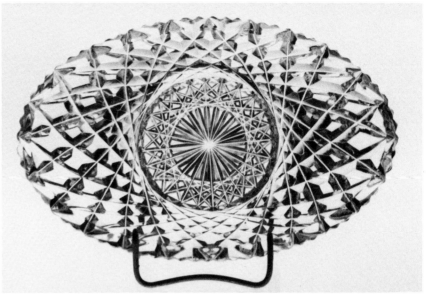

S 453. An olive dish in Garnet Pattern signed Hawkes.

C 454. An 8-inch bowl signed Hawkes in Jubilee Pattern.

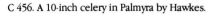

C 456. A 10-inch celery in Palmyra by Hawkes.

C 455. A coffee pot, 6.5 inches tall, in Old Irish Pattern by Hawkes.

C 457. A row outline on a 9-inch bowl in Pilgrim Pattern by Hawkes.

S 458. A 5-inch saucer in Portland Pattern signed
Hawkes.

S 459. Hawkes signed this syrup in the St. Regis
Pattern.

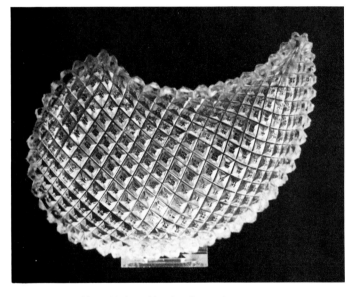

C 460. Odd shaped bonbon by Hawkes in
Strawberry Diamond.

C 461. An 8-inch bowl in Victor Pattern signed
Hawkes.

S 462. Hawkes signed this 6-inch nappy in
Cristobel Pattern. He gave this same name to
another piece with a picture of a ship in the
center.

C 463. A picture frame in Isabelle Pattern signed Hawkes.

S 464. A 6-inch, tall jug in Newport, an engraved pattern signed Hawkes.

C 465. A picture frame, 6.5 by 4.75 inches, in Strawberry Pattern signed Hawkes.

C 467. An 8-inch bowl with gothic arches in Coronet Pattern by Hawkes.

C 466. A bonbon in Pillars and Star Pattern by Hawkes.

C 468. Another gothic-arch pattern by Hawkes on a 12-inch tray in Savoy.

S 469. A saucer champagne in Colonial Pattern by Hawkes.

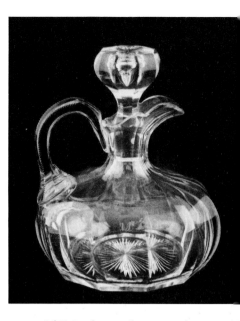

S 470. Another panel pattern in Flutes signed Hawkes.

S 471. An 8-inch bowl in Lamont Pattern signed Hawkes with panel outline.

S 472. A paneled bonbon in Mona Pattern signed Hawkes.

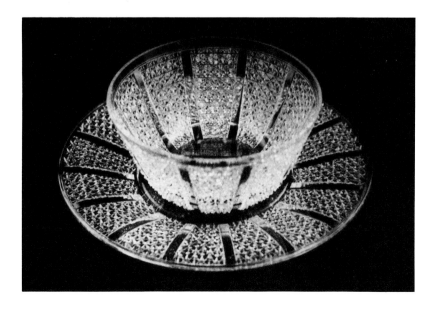

P 473. An 8-inch plate and 5.5-inch bowl of a mayonnaise set in Panel and Kohinoor by Hawkes.

474. A paneled vase, 9.5 inches tall, in Punties
nd Kohinoor by Hawkes.

C 475. A candlestick with panels in Tuetonic
Pattern signed Hawkes.

P 476. A 6.5-inch, tall jar in Victoria, signed
Hawkes.

477. Hawkes signed this 8-inch bowl cut in the
'inchester Pattern.

C 478. A 6-inch plate in a swirl design called Corn
by Hawkes.

P 479. A 12-inch tray in a swirl outline by Hawkes and named Kohinoor.

C 480. A butter plate and cover in Anson Pattern by Hawkes.

S 481. A horseradish dish, 6-inches tall, in the Arcadia Pattern by Hawkes.

S 482. An 8.5-inch, tall comport in Armanda Pattern signed Hawkes.

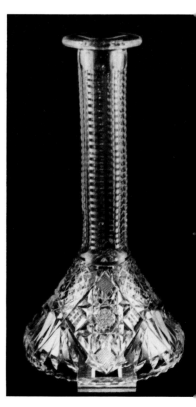

C 483. A 12-inch candlestick in Brandon Patte by Hawkes.

C 484. A vase, 12-inches tall, in Brighton Pattern signed Hawkes.

P 485. A 10.5-inch, footed bowl signed Hawkes in the Brussels Pattern.

S 486. Hawkes named this Pattern Concord.

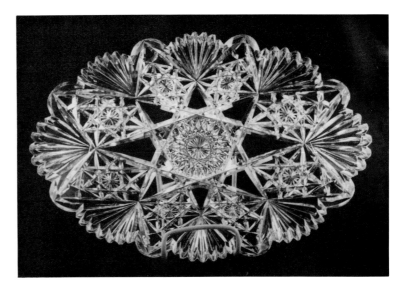

C 488. A tray, 16 by 10.5 inches, in Dorothea pattern signed Hawkes.

487. A tall champagne in Cypress Pattern by Hawkes.

C 489. A 7.5-inch, tall carafe in Florence Pattern signed Hawkes.

C 490. Hawkes named this Pattern Harold on a
10.5-inch, tall decanter.

S 491. Hawkes signed this 9-inch bowl in the
Kent Pattern.

P 492. A 5-inch saucer in Mars Pattern signed
Hawkes.

C 493. A carafe, 7.5 inches tall, in Madeline
Pattern signed Hawkes.

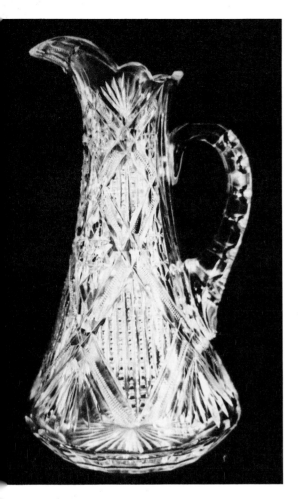

P 494. A 10-inch jug in Melrose Pattern signed Hawkes.

C 495. Hawkes named this dual motifs pattern on this 9-inch plate Mirage.

C 497. A whiskey tumbler with a sterling silver handle in New Princes by Hawkes.

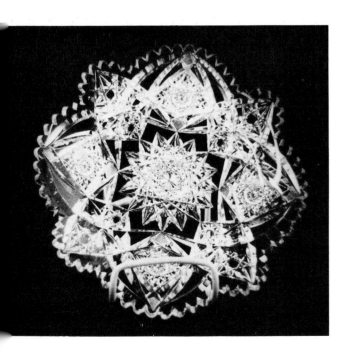

496. This 10-inch plate in Montrose Hawkes gned.

C 498. A 6-inch, tall comport in Normandy Pattern signed Hawkes.

C 499. A small flower center designated "odd" by Hawkes.

C 500. A 6-inch, tall loving cup for flowers signed Hawkes but called "Odd" in catalog.

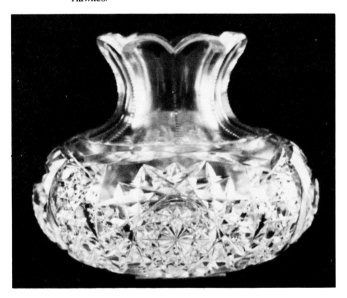

C 501. A flower center, 5-inches tall, in Premier by Hawkes.

P 503. A one-piece punch bowl in Raleigh signed Hawkes.

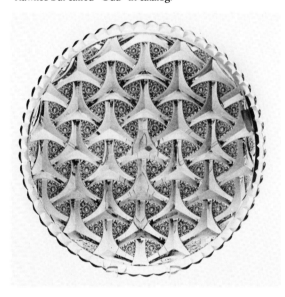

L 502. An 11-inch tray in Pueblo signed Hawkes.

C 504. Hawkes signed this 6-inch jug in Tudor Pattern.

S 505. A 10-inch decanter in the Tyrone Pattern by Hawkes.

S 506. Hawkes gave this Strawberry Diamond pattern a number, #773.

S 507. An 8-inch bowl, #2 by Hawkes has a star outline.

S 509. Hawkes signed this 7-inch plate in #1417 pattern.

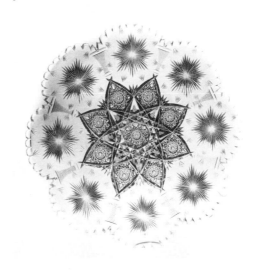

P 508. A 15-inch tray in #999 by Hawkes.

S 510. A shell bonbon in #1 Pattern by Hawkes.

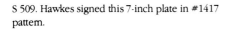

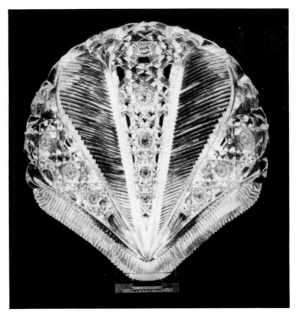

P 511. A 10-inch, crimped bowl in pattern #462 and signed Hawkes.

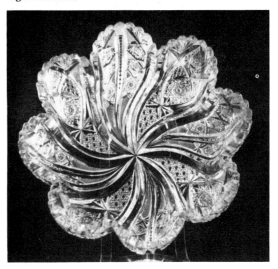

C 512. A crimped saucer in Pattern #1190 and signed Hawkes.

P 513. A 9-inch, low bowl with crimped panels in Pattern #1287 by Hawkes.

P 514. Hawkes signed this 10-inch bowl, Pattern #1302, in a swirl outline.

P 515. The Hawkes signature helped to identify this hollow center decanter as pattern #1401.

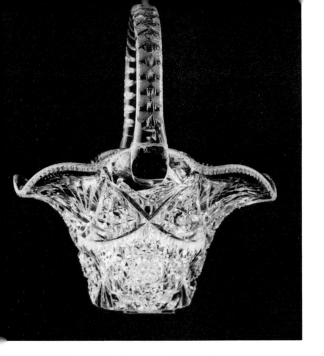

C 516. A 10-inch, tall basket in pattern #1407 and signed Hawkes.

C 517. Hawkes signed this 5-inch puff box in pattern #1582 "odd."

518. A jug and six tumblers in Hawkes' Gravic Carnation Pattern.

C 519. A 4-inch, hinged box in China Aster by Hawkes.

S 520. Hawkes called this pattern Gravic Chrysanthemum on this 8-inch bowl.

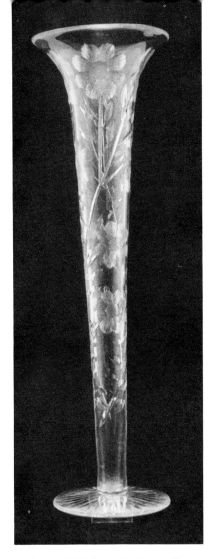

S 521. An 18.5-inch vase in Hawkes Gravic
Cosmo.

C 522. A 7-inch plate in Hawkes Gravic Dahlia.

S 523. A satin gravic design on a 9-inch plate.

C 524. A 9-inch plate in Gravic Strawberry by
Hawkes.

C 525. A two-part punch bowl in Gravic Fruit
Pattern by Hawkes.

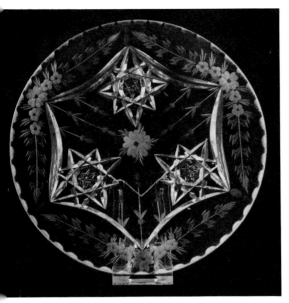

S 526. Hawkes signed this 7-inch plate and named the pattern Empire.

C 529. A 15-inch, footed vase signed Hawkes.

S 527. An engraved jug in Josephine Pattern signed Hawkes.

C 528. Hawkes signed this teapot in Napoleon 1.

C 530. An 18-inch vase in border and miter signed Hawkes.

C 531. A star outline in a 6.5-inch nappy signed Hawkes.

P 532. A 10-inch tray in a pointed loops outline with a Hawkes' signature.

C 533. A bonbon in a club shape signed Hawkes.

C 534. Hawkes signed this heart-shaped bonbon in pointed loops outline.

C 535. The matching diamond shape to the club and heart bonbon signed Hawkes.

P 536. A 10-inch, oval fruit bowl signed Hawkes.

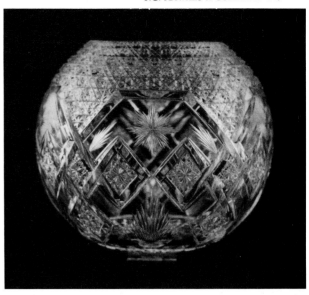

P 537. Hawkes signed this rose globe with dual motifs outline.

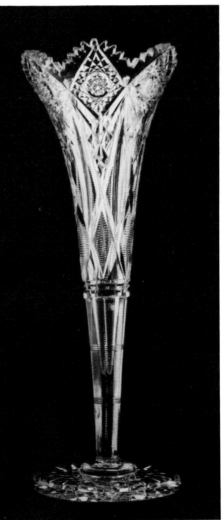

538. A 10-inch vase signed Hawkes.

C 539. A 14-inch vase signed Hawkes.

P 540. This 10-inch decanter signed Hawkes has a matching stopper.

C 541. Hawkes signed this 10-inch tray.

C 542. A 7-inch bowl signed Hawkes combined bar and circle outlines.

C 543. Hawkes signed this 14.5-inch vase in an ornate pattern.

J. HOARE & COMPANY Corning, New York 1853-1920

John Hoare immigrated from England and opened a cutting shop in New York. He later moved his shop to Corning. A very astute business man, he kept a scrapbook of his patterns on one page and those of his competitors on the opposite one (L 544). He created several patterns from the same miter outline which he numbered or named.

1. GEOMETRICS

Bars: Newport (S 545)

Border and Miter: Haydn (C 546), Hindoo (C 547), Pluto (C 548)

Star: Heron (S 549)

Panels: Rookwood (P 550), Venice (C 551)

Swirls: Crystal (P 552), Flueron (C 553)

Pointed Loops: Newport (P 554)

Dual Motifs: Champion (C 555), Delft (C 556), Eclipse (C 557), Lotus (S 558), Mecca (S 559), New York (P 560), Peerless (S 561), St. James (S 562), Tokio (S 563), Victoria (C 564)

Combinations: Jersey (S 565)

2. NUMBERED PATTERNS

Bars: #1564 (S 566), #1614 (S 567)

Border and Miter: #1917 (C 568)

Star: #932 (C 569)

Gothic Arch: #1789 (C 570), #5360 (C 571)

Panels: #1810 (S 572), #4485 (P 573), #9565 (S 574)

Pointed Loops: #770 (C 575), #1808 (S 576)

Dual Motifs: #495-regular (C 577), #548 (S 578), #1390-regular (S 579), #1818 (P 580), #1844 (C 581), #8104 (C 582), #9918-regular (S 583

3. SIGNED

Rows: footed jug (P 584)

Star: butter pat (S 585)

Dual Motifs: sauce dish (C 586), plate (S 587)

Combinations: bowl in bar and pointed loops (P 588), bowl in bar and pointed loops (C 589), jug in star and gothic arch (C 590)

S 545. A 6-inch bonbon in Oxford signed Hoare.

L 544. A page from the Hoare scrapbook showing vases.

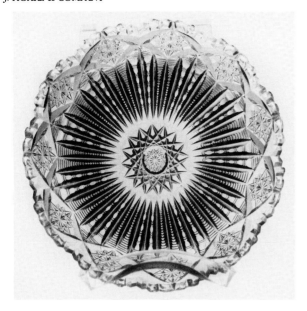

C 546. One of Hoare's border and miter outlines in an 8-inch bowl named Haydn.

C 547. An 8-inch bowl in Hindoo pattern by Hoare.

C 548. A 14-inch tray in Pluto Pattern by Hoare.

S 549. A star outline on an 8-inch bread tray in Heron by Hoare.

P 550. A footed jug, 12-inches tall, in Rookwood Pattern by Hoare.

C 551. An 8-inch bowl in Venice Pattern by Hoare.

C 553. Hoare called the pattern on this 8-inch bowl Flueron.

554. A two-part punch bowl, 12.5 by 11.5 inches, in Newport Pattern by Hoare.

P 552. A 10-inch decanter in Crystal Pattern by Hoare uses a swirl outline.

C 555. A 10.5-inch decanter in Champion Pattern by Hoare.

C 556. A dinner bell in Delft Pattern by Hoare.

C 557. A cheese plate and cover in Eclipse Pattern by Hoare.

S 558. An oil in Lotus Pattern by Hoare.

S 559. A medium-sized sugar and cream in Mecca Pattern by Hoare.

P 560. An 8-inch, tall jug in New York Pattern by Hoare.

S 561. Hoare signed this 8-inch, tall comport in Peerless.

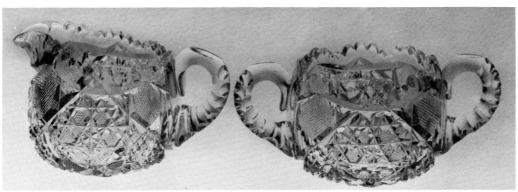

S 563. Hoare designated the pattern Tokio on this 8-inch bowl.

S 562. A 9-inch, tall jug in St. James Pattern signed Hoare.

S 564. An 11-inch decanter in Victoria Pattern by Hoare.

S 565. In Jersey Pattern on a 6-inch nappy Hoare combined border with star outline.

S 566. A 10-inch bowl in Pattern #1564 signed Hoare.

S 567. Hoare signed this 8-inch bowl in pattern #1614.

C 568. A 12-inch vase in pattern #1917 by Hoare.

C 569. A 7-inch plate in pattern #932 by Hoare.

C 570. Hoare numbered this pattern #1789 on a 7-inch spoon tray.

C 571. A 9-inch bowl in pattern #5360 by Hoare.

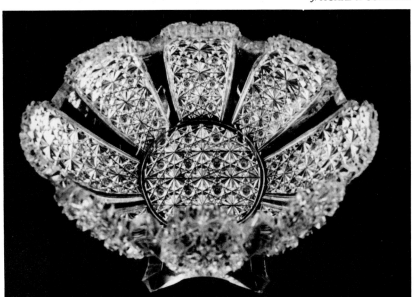

S 572. Hoare signed this 7-inch plate in pattern #1810.

P 573. An oval fruit bowl, 11 by 8 inches, in Russian or pattern #4485 by Hoare.

C 575. Pattern #770 identified this 8-inch, tall jug by Hoare in pointed loops outline.

S 574. A 9-inch candlestick in pattern #9565 by Hoare.

S 576. A 7-inch spoon tray in pattern #1808 by Hoare.

C 577. A cigar jar in pattern #495-regular by
Hoare.

S 578. A 12 by 14-inch punch bowl in pattern
#548 by Hoare.

S 579. A flower jar, 5 by 5.5 inches, in pattern
#1390-regular by Hoare.

P 580. A two-part punch bowl, 16 by 13 inches, in
pattern #1811 by Hoare.

C 581. A 10-inch plate by Hoare in pattern #1844.

582. Hoare designated this 6-inch bonbon as pattern #8104.

S 583. A 5.5-inch vase in pattern #9918-regular by Hoare.

S 585. A 3.5-inch butter pat in a star outline by Hoare.

S 586. A sauce set signed by Hoare.

584. Hoare signed this 10-inch tall jug.

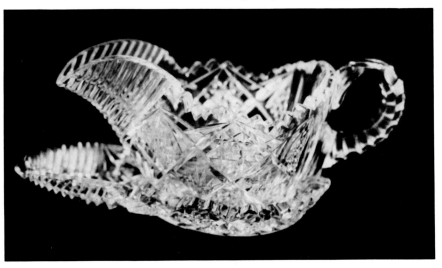

S 587. Hoare signed this 7-inch plate.

P 588. Hoare signed this 10-inch bowl in a bar and pointed loops outline.

C 589. A 9-inch bowl in bar and pointed loops outline signed Hoare.

C 590. A 7-inch jug combined outlines of star and gothic arch, signed Hoare.

LIBBEY GLASS COMPANY Toledo, Ohio 1888-1925

W. L. Libbey and his son Edward Drummon founded this factory after the dissolution of the New England Glass Company. They eventually moved the factory to Toledo. Libbey did not sell three shapes in blanks to cutting shop as previous mentioned: a tall jug with a blunt lip, a whiskey jug with a basket handle (P 591), or a decanter with a bulging neck (P 592).

From the very beginning the company covered the blank with ornate patterns. A number of patterns included a star (S 593). Late in the Brilliant Period the company used figured blanks (L 594) and did little cutting on them (S 595). The production of the company rivaled that of Hawkes.

1. GEOMETRICS
  Rows: Patent #19,165 (S 596), Star (P 597), Toledo (C 598), Zenobia (S 599)
  Border and Miter: Empress (P 600), Radiant (S 601)
  Star: Fleur-De-Lis (C 602), Gem (S 603), Melrose (S 604)
  Gothic Arch: Diana (C 605), Grand Prize (P 606)
  Panels: Cut Flute (S 607), Morello (C 608)
  Pointed Loops: Anita (S 609), Azora (C 610)
  Dual Motifs: Corena (P 611), Iola (C 612), Montrose (P 613), Nassau (C 514), Zenda (S 615)
  Combinations: Rosella in bar and star (P 616)

2. NUMBERED PATTERNS
  Border and Miter: #48 (S 617), #88 (C 618), #181 without nailhead diamond (P 619)
  Panels: #406 ((S 620), #826 (S 621)
  Pointed Loops: #25 (C 622)
  Dual Motifs: #69 (C 623), #82 (C 624), #105 (S 625), #129 (C 626), #164 (S 627), #202 (P 628)

3. SIGNED
  Bars: bowl with vertical bars (S 629)
  Border and Miter: double border jug (C 630), plate with crosshatched border (C 631)
  Star: bread tray (S 632), crimped bowl (C 633)
  Gothic Arch: bowl (P 634)
  Dual Motifs: squat decanter (C 635), vase (C 636)
  Combinations: nappy in border and miter with star centers (S 637)

4. FLORAL
  #171 Engraved (P 638), #171 Engraved (C 639), #519 Engraved (C 640), #546 Engraved (C 641)
  Signed: tray (C 642), bowl with thistle C 643), bowl with flowers (S 644)

P 591. A whiskey jug in Fern Pattern by Libbey.

C 592. A 12-inch decanter with a bulbous neck signed Libbey.

S 593. Libbey used a star outline and frequently covered the entire blank as in this signed, 7-inch plate.

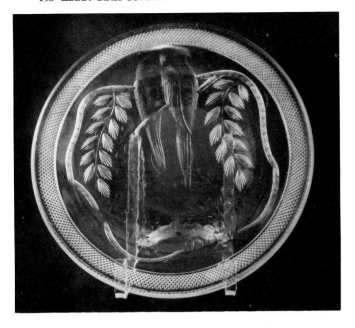

S 594. Late in the Brilliant Period, Libbey used figured blanks as illustrated by this one for Wisteria Pattern.

S 595. A 9-inch plate in the Wisteria Pattern signed Libbey.

S 596. A square nappy 6.5 inches, in a row pattern, Patent #19105.

P 597. A 10-inch tray in Star Pattern signed Libbey follows the row outline.

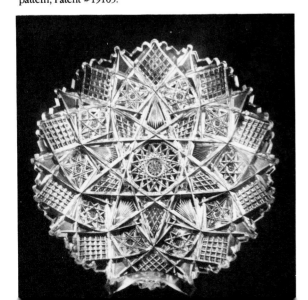

C 598. A 12-inch tray in Toledo Pattern signed Libbey.

C 599. A row outline in a vase, 13 inches, in Zenoba Pattern by Libbey.

S 601. Libbey signed this 6-inch nappy in Radiant Pattern.

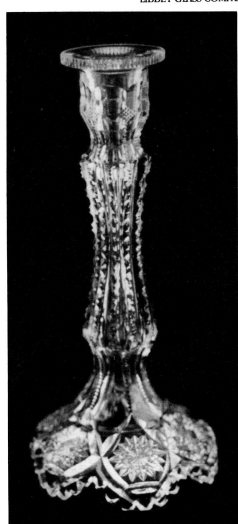

P 600. A 12-inch candlestick in Empress signed Libbey uses the border and miter outline.

S 602. A loving cup, 7-inches tall, in Fleur De Lis Pattern by Libbey.

S 603. Libbey signed this 6-inch nappy in Gem Pattern.

S 604. A 7-inch plate in Melrose Pattern by Libbey.

C 605. Libbey signed this 10-inch, square tray in Diana.

P 606. A 10-inch bowl in Grand Prize Pattern by Libbey outlined in gothic arches.

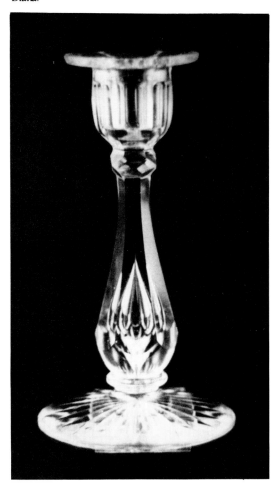

S 607. A 7-inch candlestick in Cut Flute Pattern signed Libbey.

C 608. Libbey named this 12.5-inch tray in Morello, a panel pattern.

S 609. Libbey signed this 5-inch nappy in the Anita Pattern with pointed loops.

C 610. A 7-inch tall comport in Azora Pattern by Libbey with dual motifs.

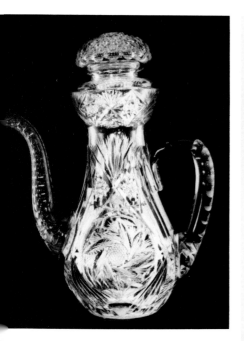

611. A coffee pot in Corena Pattern by Libbey.

C 612. An 11-inch, tall jug in Iola Pattern signed Libbey.

P 613. A basket, 14 inched tall, in Montrose Pattern by Libbey.

14. A small sugar and cream in Nassau tern by Libbey.

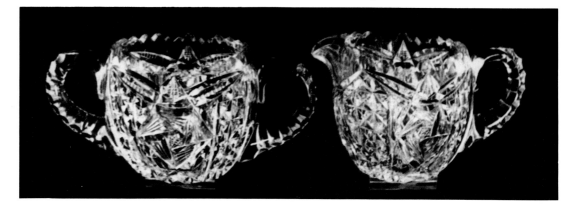

S 615. Libbey signed this 8-inch, tall jug in Zenda.

P 616. An oval, fruit bowl, 12-inches, in Rosella Pattern signed Libbey.

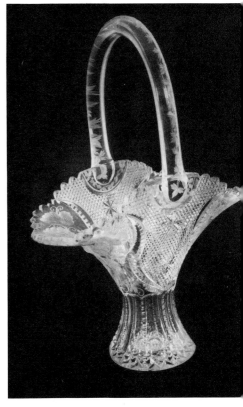

C 618. A 13-inch tall basket in pattern #88 signed Libbey.

S 617. A tooth-powder bottle in pattern #48 by Libbey.

P 619. An 18-inch tall basket in pattern #181 signed Libbey, but catalog does not show nailhead diamonds.

S 620. A leaf-shaped bonbon, 4.5 by 2.75, in pattern #406 signed Libbey.

S 621. A 9-inch candlestick in pattern #826 by Libbey.

C 622. A flower center, 8-inches tall, in pattern #25 by Libbey.

C 623. A grape fruit holder and liner reversed so as to show it better, in pattern #69 by Libbey.

C 624. A catsup bottle, 6.5 inches, in pattern #82 signed Libbey.

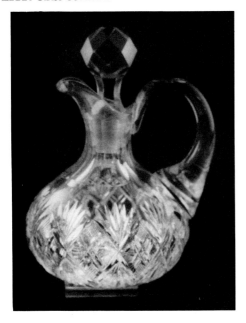

S 625. A 6-inch oil in pattern #105 by Libbey.

C 626. A plate and covered cheese in pattern #129 by Libbey.

S 627. An 8-inch tall jug in pattern #164 signed Libbey on top of handle.

P 628. A footed, oval fruit bowl in pattern #202 and signed Libbey.

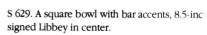

S 629. A square bowl with bar accents, 8.5-inc signed Libbey in center.

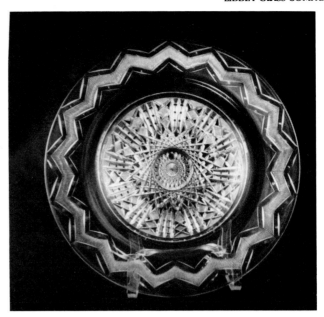

C 630. An 8.5-inch, tall jug signed Libbey with with triple borders.

C 631. A 10-inch plate with a border around a center of notched miters and crosshatched diamonds, signed Libbey.

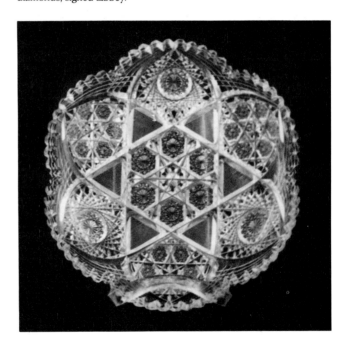

632. A bread tray, 8 by 5 inches, in star outline nd signed Libbey.

C 633. A 9-inch low bowl in a star outline, signed Libbey.

P 634. A 10-inch bowl with gothic arches signed Libbey.

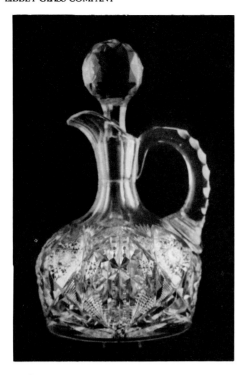

C 635. A decanter, 9.5 inches tall, in dual motifs outline, signed Libbey.

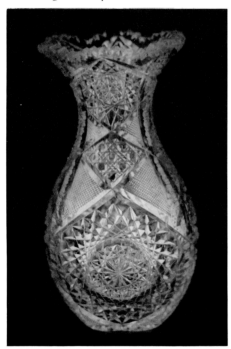

C 636. An 8-inch vase signed Libbey.

C 639. Libbey signed this 10-inch plate in #174 Engraved.

C 637. Libbey signed this 6-inch nappy that combined border and bar outline.

P 638. This 14-inch punch bowl Libbey signed and listed as #171 Engraved.

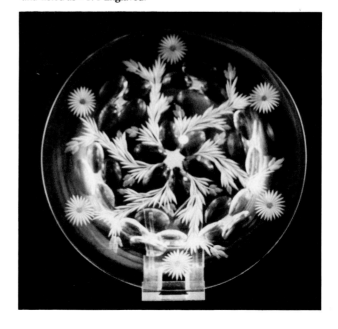

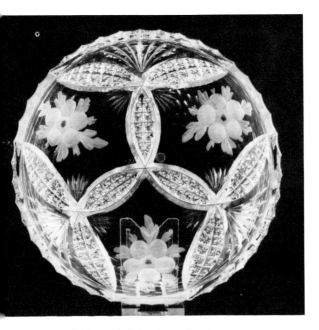

C 640. A 7-inch bowl signed Libbey in #519 Engraved.

C 641. Libbey signed this 9-inch jug in #546 Engraved.

C 642. A 9-inch low bowl in star outline signed Libbey.

C 643. A thistle center dominates this 6.5-inch plate signed Libbey.

S 644. An 8-inch bowl cut in flowers and signed Libbey.

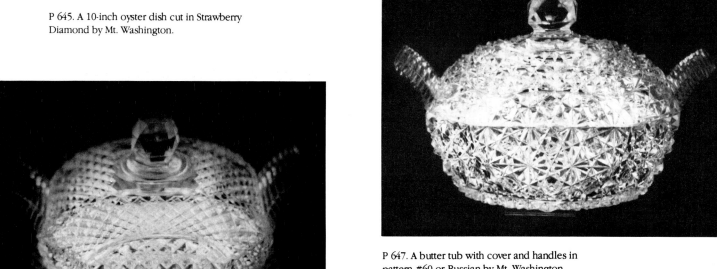

P 645. A 10-inch oyster dish cut in Strawberry Diamond by Mt. Washington.

MOUNT WASHINGTON GLASS WORKS New Bedford, Massachusetts 1837-1894
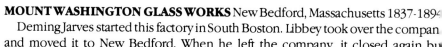
Deming Jarves started this factory in South Boston. Libbey took over the compan and moved it to New Bedford. When he left the company, it closed again bu reopened two years later in 1876. In 1894 the Pairpoint Corporation absorbed it.

Some of the odd shapes catch the fancy of the collector: oyster dish (P 645), plat and covered butter (P 646), and covered butter tub (P 647). Other oddities include Hungarian vase (P 648) and a centerpiece, but a collector found only the bird an not the two wings (P 649). The company boxed a set of four pin trays (S 650).

Rows: Hortensia (C 651), Radiant (C 652), Regent (C 653), Westminister (C 654
Star: Corinthian (C 655)
Pointed Loops: Holland (C 656)

P 646. An 8-inch plate and cover for butter with handles by Mt. Washington.

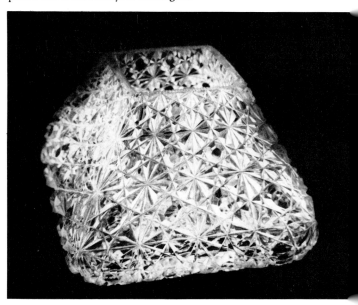

P 647. A butter tub with cover and handles in pattern #60 or Russian by Mt. Washington.

P 648. A 7-inch tall Hungarian vase in pattern #60 by Mt. Washington.

P 649. The body of a three piece bird set, two wings missing by Mt. Washington in #60 Pattern.

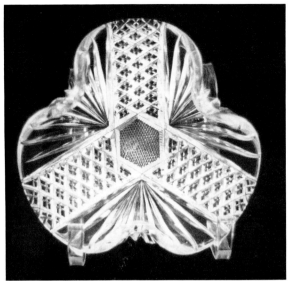

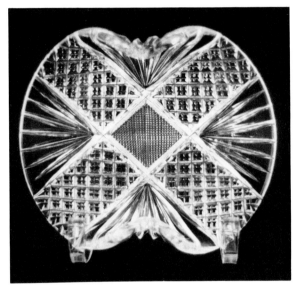

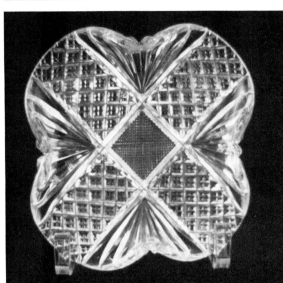

S 650. A boxed set of pin trays cut by Mt. Washington in bar outline.

C 651. An 8-inch carafe in Hortensia by Mt. Washington.

C 652. A champagne in Radiant Pattern by Mt. Washington.

C 654. A spoon tray, 5.5 by 4 inches, in Westminister by Mt. Washington.

C 653. A 9-inch, tall jug in Regent Pattern by Mt. Washington.

C 655. A 9-inch, square dish in Corinthian Pattern by Mt. Washington.

C 656. A 10-inch dresser tray in Holland Pattern by Mt. Washington.

PAIRPOINT CORPORATION New Bedford, Massachusetts 1880-1938

In 1880, Mt. Washington organized the Pairpoint Corporation to make silver mountings. When Mt. Washington closed, Pairpoint took over the company. The company produced some unusual items, such as this decanter (P 657) and this covered mushroom dish (P 658). The pieces in Raised diamond came in the late Brilliant Period (C 659).

1. GEOMETRICS
  Bars: Jeanette (P 660)
  Rows: Adelaide (C 661), Berkshire (C 662)
  Star: Pearl (jewel) (C 663), Pearl (jewel) (C 664), Pearl (handkerchief) (C 665), Pearl (glove) (C 666)
  Panels: Estelle (C 667), Odd (C 668)
  Circles: Mistletoe (P 669)
  Dual Motifs: Baltic (S 670), Caldonia (S 471), Cactus (S 672), Huron (C 673), Idlewild (C 674), Loraine (P 675), Palmetto (S 676), Pioneer (C 677), Punty and Raised Diamond (C 678), Rustic (C 679), Tokay (C 680), Uncatena (C 681)

2. FLORALS AND FRUIT
  Acorn (C 682), Brazil (S 683), Colias (C 684), Diamond (S 685), Garland (C 686), Moth (C 687), Stratford (S 688) Engraved Grape (C 689), Engraved #134 (C 690), Engraved #141 (C 691)

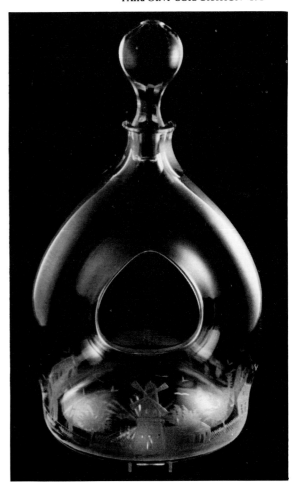

P 657. A 12-inch decanter in Beldon Pattern by Pairpoint.

P 658. A mushroom set in Raised Diamond by Pairpoint.

C 659. A footed fruit bowl in Raised Diamond Pattern by Pairpoint.

P 660. An 8.5-inch, tall urn in Jeanette Pattern by Pairpoint with bars separating the hobstars.

C 662. A 6-inch sugar shaker in Berkshire Pattern by Pairpoint in row outline.

C 661. A 9-inch horn-of-plenty vase on an orb in Pairpoint's Adelaide Pattern.

C 663. In this later version of a jewel box Pairpoint used parallel miters on the bowl part of this pattern in Pearl.

C 664. In an earlier pattern of Pearl, a Pairpoint catalog showed the lower part cut with rows of punties.

C 665. A 6-inch square handkerchief box in Pearl
Pattern with punties by Pairpoint.

C 666. A glove box, 10 by 4 inches, in Pearl
matches the other two dresser pieces by
Pairpoint.

C 667. A 9-inch, crimped bowl in Estelle Pattern
by Pairpoint.

P 669. A low bowl, 14 by 10 inches, in Mistletoe
Pattern by Pairpoint, a circle outline.

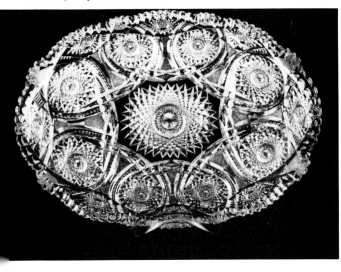

C 668. A 10-inch vase designated Odd in
Pairpoint catalog.

S 670. A 6-inch, calling card tray in Baltic by Pairpoint.

S 671. A 10-inch cheese and cracker tray in Caldonia Pattern by Pairpoint.

S 672. A 5 by 5-inch vase in Cactus Pattern by Pairpoint.

S 673. Pairpoint named this 8-inch olive Huron.

C 674. A 9-inch tall jug in Idlewild Pattern by Pairpoint.

S 676. An 8-inch bowl in Palmetto Pattern by Pairpoint.

P 675. A two-handled, center piece, 13 inches tall, in Loraine Pattern by Pairpoint.

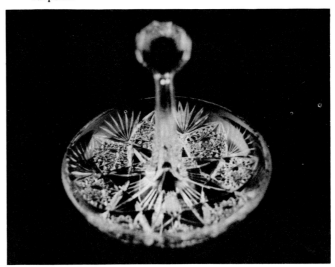

C 677. A 6-inch bonbon with center handle in Pioneer Pattern by Pairpoint.

C 679. A 7-inch plate in Rustic Pattern by Pairpoint.

C 678. Pairpoint called this pattern on a 9-inch, tall jug Punty and Raised Diamond.

C 680. A finger bowl, 4.5 inches, in Tokay Pattern by by Pairpoint.

C 682. A ten-inch plate in Acorn Pattern by Pairpoint.

S 683. A 10.5-inch, punch server in Brazil Pattern by Pairpoint.

C 681. A 9-inch, tall flower holder with insert in Uncatena Pattern by Pairpoint.

C 684. Pairpoint engraved this 9-inch, tall comport in Colias Pattern.

S 685. A 7-inch spoon tray in Diamond Pattern by Pairpoint, cut on a figured blank.

C 686. A 4-inch, tall comport on a figured blank in Garland Pattern by Pairpoint.

C 687. An 8-inch bowl in Moth Pattern by Pairpoint.

S 688. A 10-inch cheese and cracker dish in Stratford.

C 689. Pairpoint called this pattern on a 12-inch jug Engraved Grapes.

C 690. A 10-inch plate Pairpoint designated as
Engraved #134.

C 691. Pairpoint named this pattern on a 7-inch
relish Engraved #141.

S 692. A 9-inch dish in Japan by Pitkin & Brooks.

PITKIN & BROOKS Chicago, Illinois 1872-ca. 1920

Edward H. Pitkin and Jonathan W. Brooks organized this factory and became one of the largest wholesale distributors. The catalog, as previously mentioned, stated the company produced three types of glass: that sent to Europe for cutting, that equal to their competitors, and a quality grade they signed.

Bars: Japan (S 692), #263 (C 693)

Border and Miter: Diamond (C 694), #348 (C 695)

Star: Mars (P 696)

Gothic Arch: Eldorado (C 697), Halle (C 698)

Swirls: Carnegie (C 699)

Pointed Loops: Carolyn (C 700), Garland (P 701), Mayflower (P 702)

Dual Motifs: Angelo (C 703), Arams (C 704), Byrns (C 705), Corsair (S 706), Daisy (C 707), Metropole (C 708), Osborne (S 709), St Regis (C 710), Spillane (S 711), Triumph (S 712)

Signed: tray (P 713)

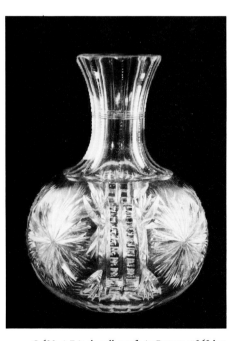

C 693. A 7-inch, tall carafe in Pattern #262 by
Pitkin & Brooks.

C 694. A whiskey bottle, 10 inches, in Diamond
by Pitkin & Brooks.

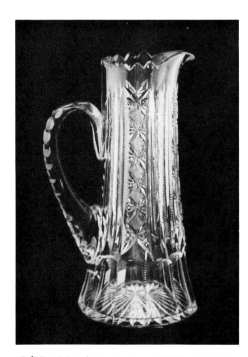

C 695. A 9.5-inch jug in pattern #348 by Pitkin &
Brooks.

C 696. A pointed loop outline on this 12-inch tray in Mars by Pitkin & Brooks.

C 697. A 9-inch bowl in Eldorado by Pitkin & Brooks.

C 698. An oval, fruit bowl, 8 by 6.5 inches, in Halle Pattern by Pitkin & Brooks.

C 700. A jug 8-inches tall, in a pointed loop pattern called Carolyn signed Pitkin & Brooks.

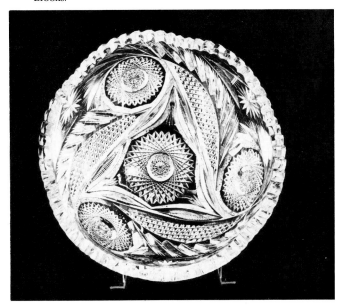

C 699. An 8-inch bowl in Carnegie pattern by Pitkin & Brooks in a swirl outline.

P 701. A 10-inch bowl in Garland Pattern by Pitkin & Brooks.

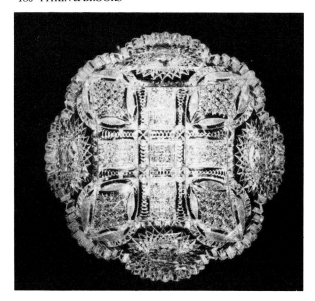

P 702. A low bowl, 9 inches, in Mayflower Pattern by Pitkin & Brooks.

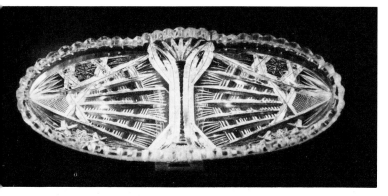

C 704. Arans Pattern on a 11.75-inch celery, signed Pitkin & Brooks.

S 706. A 4-inch, tall comport signed Pitkin & Brooks in Corsair Pattern.

C 703. Pitkin & Brooks signed this footed sugar and cream in Angelo Pattern.

C 705. A footed sugar and cream in Byrns Pattern by Pitkin & Brooks.

C 707. A basket, 12 inches tall, in Daisy and signed Pitkin & Brooks.

C 708. A 7-inch relish with a center handle in Metropole Pattern signed Pitkin & Brooks.

S 709. An olive, 4.5 inches, in Osborne by Pitkin & Brooks.

C 710. A 6-inch mayonnaise bowl in St. Regis Pattern by Pitkin & Brooks.

S 711. A 6-inch, spoon tray in Spillane Pattern by Pitkin & Brooks.

S 712. A flower center, 12-inches in diameter, in Triumph Pattern by Pitkin & Brooks.

P 713. Pitkin & Brooks signed this 10-inch, oval tray.

L 714. A figured blank Sinclare used.

S 715. A 9-inch bowl in Mitre and Lattice by Sinclaire.

P 716. Sinclaire gave this row pattern in a 10-inch, square bowl number #98.

H. P. SINCLAIRE & COMPANY Corning, New York 1904-1928

Sinclaire worked for Hawkes before organizing his cutting shop. He designed some very outstanding geometrics design, but, as a naturalist, he produced much engraved glass. A geometric design often received an engraved floral border. He designed a number of patterns with medallions for flowers. Even Sinclaire eventually used figured blanks (L 714).

1. GEOMETRICS
   Rows: Mitre and Lattice (S 615), #98 (P 716)
   Border and Miter: Belfast (P 717), Charter (P 718), Florentine (S 719), Prism (P 720), #1028 (C 721)
   Panels: Ontario (C 722)
   Pointed Loops: # 1021 (C 723)
   Dual Motifs: Brussels (P 724), Cumberland (C 725), Spartan (S 726)
2. SIGNED
   Bars: Bowl (C 727)
   Gothic Arch: six-sided bowl (C 728)
   Dual Motifs: bowl (C 729)
3. ENGRAVED PATTERNS
   Floral: Adelphia (S 730), Millicent (C 731)
   Fruit: Assyrian and Strawberries (P 732)
   Signed: basket (C 733)

P 718. Sinclaire named the pattern on this 9-inch bottle Charter.

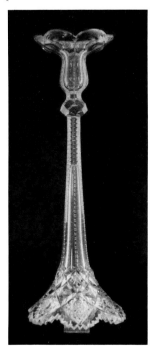

P 717. An 18-inch candlestick in Belfast and signed Sinclaire.

S 719. A 6.5-inch plate in Florentine with a border and miter outline by Sinclaire.

P 720. Sinclaire cut medallions in the border of
this pattern in Prism.

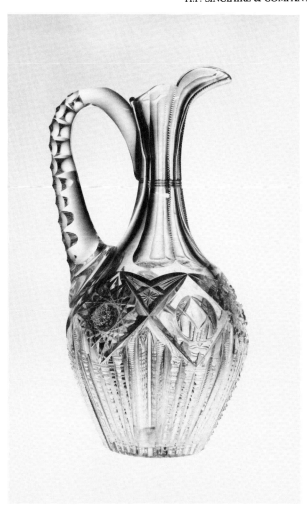

C 721. A 14-inch jug in pattern #1028 by Sinclaire.

C 723. A 10-inch bowl in pattern #1021 by
Sinclaire uses a pointed-loop outline.

C 722. A 7.5-inch bottle in Ontario Pattern signed
Sinclaire.

C 724. Sinclaire signed this 9-inch, tall jug in Brussels Pattern.

C 725. A whiskey tumbler in Sinclaire's Cumberland Pattern.

S 726. A 6.5-inch nappy in Spartan Pattern signed Sinclaire.

C 727. A bar outline on a 9-inch bowl signed Sinclaire.

C 728. A 9-inch bowl in a gothic arch outline signed Sinclaire.

C 729. Sinclaire signed this 10-inch bowl in a dual motifs outline.

S 730. A 10-inch tray in Adelphia by Sinclaire.

C 731. A jug with medallions for flowers in Millicent Pattern signed Sinclaire.

P 732. Sinclaire named this pattern Assyrian and Strawberries.

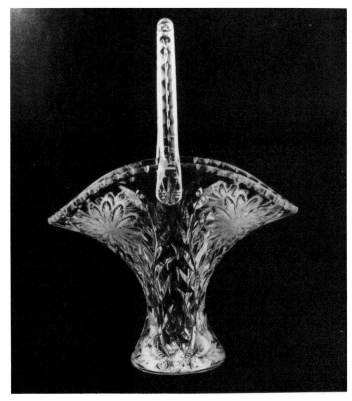

C 733. A basket signed Sinclaire.

P 734. An 18-inch lamp in Cut Rose Pattern by Tuthill.

P 735. An 8-inch bowl in star outline signed Tuthill.

P 736. A 10-inch tray in Wheel Pattern by Tuthill.

TUTHILL CUT GLASS COMPANY Middletown, New York 1894-1923

Charles Tuthill first opened a shop in Corning and cut geometric patterns comparable to those of Hawkes or Hoare. When he moved his cutting shop to Middletown, he began to do patterns in geometrics and intaglio or intaglio only (C 734). See *Identifying American Brilliant Cut Glass* where the Tuthill patterns are shown in detail.

Star: signed bowl (P 735)

Panels: Wheel (P 736), signed plate (P 737)

Dual Motifs: signed tray (C 738), tumbler (C 739) comport (C 740).

The patterns in this chapter become a source of reference to help you with unidentified pieces or making a "buy" list. Mostly you will learn the names of patterns on your glass and a few others. If you have not identified all your patterns, you may find them with these additional sources.

P 737. A 6-inch nappy signed Tuthill in panels.

C 738. A 10-inch plate signed Tuthill in dual motifs outline.

C 739. A tumbler signed Tuthill.

C 740. A comport with weighted base in dual motif outline signed Tuthill.

Chapter 7 *Additional Sources of Pattern Identification*

With the increasing demand for cut glass, older companies took on new functions, and new businesses developed in the production and selling areas. Some of these companies published catalogs, advertised in magazines, and even used a signature. So if you need to find an identity for a piece of cut glass in your collection, consider the following sources.

We listed only those companies whose cut glass we found in collections.

LESSER-KNOWN CUT GLASS COMPANIES

Frequently a cutter at a major company opened his own shop or a family operated a business. Several business men often formed a company.

ALMY & THOMAS Corning, New York 1903-1907

This company produced a general line of cut glass in geometric patterns. With no available catalog only an acid-etched signature provided the identification for the source as with this piece in a pointed loop pattern (C 741).

BLACKMER CUT GLASS COMPANY New Bedford, Massachusetts 1894-1916

Authur L. Blackmer first worked in the office of the Mt. Washington Glass Works before he established his own cutting shop. He published two catalogs and perhaps more that illustrated basic, geometric patterns.

Bars: Homer (C 742), Fremont (C 743), Zephyr (C 744)
Rows: Lyndale (C 745)
Panels: Comstellation (C 746)
Gothic Arch: Nordica (P 747), Pricilla (S 748)
Dual Motifs: Cosair (C 749), Eclipse (750), Prudence (C 751)

C 741. A 14.5-inch tray in a pointed loop outline signed Almy & Thomas.

C 744. The pattern on a 12-inch ice cream tray Blackmer named Zephyr.

C 745. A 7-inch bowl in Lyndale Pattern by Blackmer.

C 742. Blackmer cut this 10-inch tray in the Homer Pattern.

C 743. The Fremont Pattern by Blackmer decorates this 16-inch, decanter.

P 747. Blackmer cut the Nordica Pattern on this 9-inch bowl.

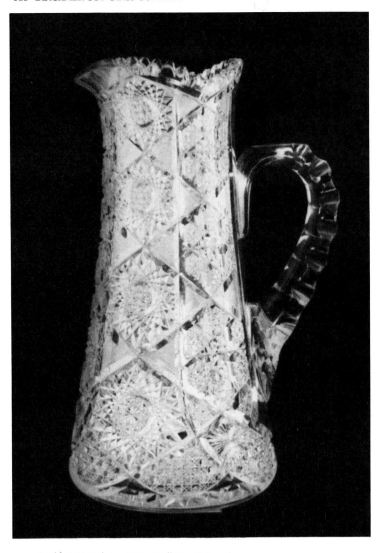

C 746. A 12-inch jug in Constellation Pattern by Blackmer.

S 748. A comport in Pricilla Pattern by Blackmer.

S 749. A 9-inch, tall comport in Corsair Pattern by Blackmer.

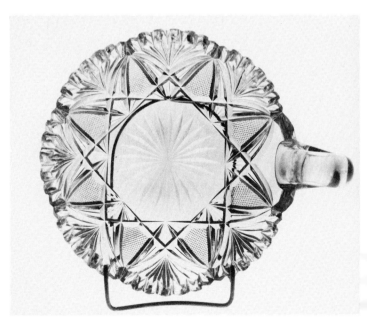

S 750. A 6-inch nappy in the Eclipse Pattern by Blackmer.

C 751. An orange bowl, 8 by 5 inches, in
Prudence Pattern by Blackmer.

ELMIRA GLASS COMPANY Corning, New York ca. 1903-1914

This cutting shop bought blanks from Doflinger and Pairpoint. In the one catalog
preserved, the company numbered all the patterns. Some duplicated those of larger
companies where patents had expired.

Bars: #33 (S 752)
Star: #80 (C 753)
Gothic Arch: #51 (C 754)
Dual Motifs: #3 (C 755), #18 (P 756), #67 (C 757), #100 (C 758)

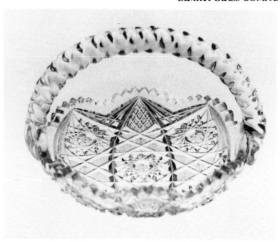

S 752. A 7-inch diameter basket in pattern #33 by
Elmira.

C 753. An 8-inch, crimped bowl in pattern #80 by
Elmira.

C 754. An 8-inch bowl in Elmira pattern #51, a
gothic arch outline.

P 756. A comport, 10 inches tall, in pattern #18 by
Elmira.

C 755. Elmira numbered this vase #3.

C 757. An 8-inch, tall comport in pattern #67 by Elmira.

C 758. A 7-inch butter cover and plate by Elmira in pattern #100.

C 759. A 4-inch whiskey tumbler signed Hope.

S 760. Hope also signed this shot glass.

HOPE GLASS WORKS Providence, Rhode Island 1872-1951

To date no one has found a catalog published by this cutting shop. The company did patent an acid-etched signature (See appendix). We found two signed pieces: a whiskey tumbler (C 759) and a shot glass (S 760)

IDEAL CUT GLASS COMPANY Syracuse, New York 1903-1933

This cutting shop organized in Corning but moved to Syracuse in 1904. Most collectors associate the company with the Poinsetta Pattern (S 761). A covered, six-sided box used parallel miters and a floral design on the lid (S 762). The company bought blanks from Pairpoint, Union, Libbey, and Fry and sold to east coast jewelry and department stores.

S 761. A double-handled nappy in the Poinsettia Pattern by Ideal.

S 762. A 6-sided, covered box in a floral pattern by Ideal.

S 763. Irving signed this 8-inch bowl in Harvard Pattern.

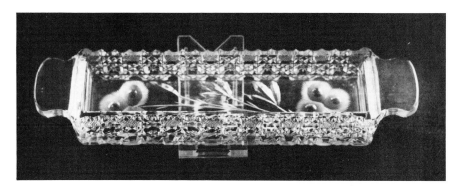

S 764. An 8.5-inch domino sugar in Capital Pattern by Irving.

IRVING CUT GLASS COMPANY, INC. Honesdale, Pennsylvania 1900-1930

William H. Hawken, a pattern maker, and five other men formed this company which worked mostly on figured blanks purchased from Fry. The company conducted an extensive mail order business in South Africa, Spain, China, and Japan.

Star: Harvard (S 763)

Florals: Capital (S 764), Combination Rose (C 765), Daisy (S 766), White Rose (C 767)

Signed: pickle (S 768)

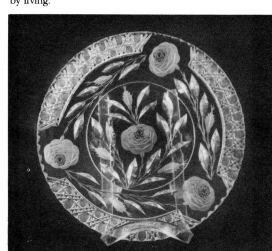

C 766. Irving signed this 10-inch plate in Combination Rose Pattern

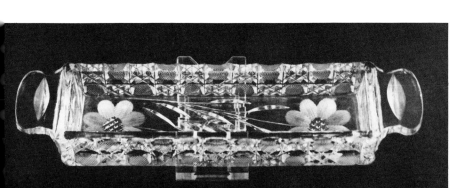

S 765. An 8.5-inch domino sugar in Daisy Pattern by Irving.

C 767. An 8-inch plate in White Rose Pattern by Irving.

S 768. Irving signed this 8-inch pickle dish.

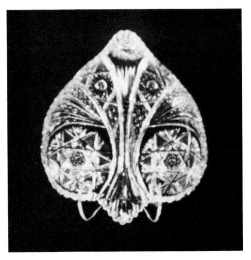

S 769. Krantz-Smith named the pattern on this bonbon Alicia.

C 770. A six-inch, tall cherry jar in Iowa Pattern Krantz-Smith.

S 771. Lackwanna named this pattern on a carafe Marion.

S 772. An 8-inch bowl in Beryl Pattern by Laurel.

P 773. An 18-inch, tall lamp in Celandine Pattern by Laurel.

KRANTZ-SMITH & COMPANY Honesdale, Pennsylvania 1893-1932

T. B. Tinker, a wholesaler in Chicago, published several catalogs with a few pages with illustrations from this company's cut glass. Two pattern identifications include a circle outline in Alicia (S 769) and a cherry bottle in Iowa (C 770).

LACKAWANNA CUT GLASS COMPANY Scranton, Pennsylvania 1903-1905

This cutting shop sold cut glass primarily by mail on a money back guarantee if not satisfied. The company signed glass and published a catalog that related facts about shapes and identified patterns as this one in Marion (S 771).

LAUREL CUT GLASS COMPANY Jermyn, Pennsylvania 1903-1920

The Laurel Cut Glass Company first used the name German Cut Glass Company, then changed it to Laurel, to Kohinur, and finally back to Laurel. The company, one of a very few, hired women as cutters and polishers. Two different catalogs illustrated the following patterns:

Bars: Beryl (S 772), Celandine (P 773)

Star: Athens (P 774)

Pointed Loops: Vittoria (C 775)

Dual Motifs: Cleopatria (C 776), Marcia (C 777), Neptune (S 778), Optimo (S 779), Ortrud (C 780)

Combinations: Triumph (C 781)

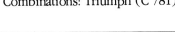

P 774. A 10-inch, low bowl with a star outline in Athens Pattern by Laurel.

C 775. Laurel named this pattern Vittoria on a relish with curved sides.

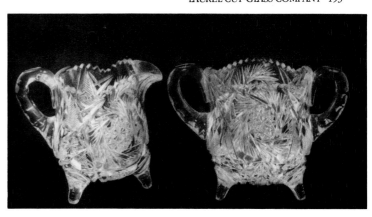

C 776. A sugar and cream in Cleopatria Pattern by Laurel.

C 777. A footed, fruit bowl, 9 by 5 inches, in Marcia Pattern by Laurel.

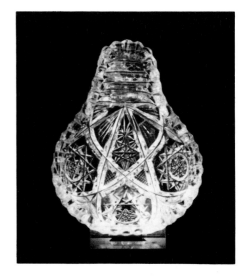

C 778. A butter pat with a handle in Neptune Pattern by Laurel.

C 779. A 6-inch nappy in Optimo Pattern by Laurel.

C 780. Laurel named this pattern Ortrud cut on a cracker jar.

C 781. An 8-inch bowl in Triumph Pattern by Laurel.

C 783. Luzerne signed this 8-inch whiskey decanter in Laurette Pattern.

LUZERNE CUT GLASS COMPANY Pittston, Pennslyvania Ca. 1918-1930

A catalog from this cutting shop identifies a bar pattern as Olga (C 782) and a dual motifs one as Laurette (C 783).

MAPLE CITY GLASS COMPANY Hawley, Pennsylvania 1900-1911

John S. O'Connor organized this cutting shop and then sold it to Maple City Cut Glass Company in 1900. The company published ten catalogs before Clark bought it.

Rows: Temple (P 784)

Gothic Arch: Altair (C 785), Crafton (C 786), Marswell (C 787)

Dual Motifs: Bonita (C 788), Dodona (C 789), Nirvana (S 790), Roma (C 791), Sunbeam (S 792)

Combinations: Kenwood (C 793)

Signed: Border and Miter vase (C 794)

C 782. An 11-inch vase in Olga Pattern by Luzerne.

C 785. Maple City signed this 8-inch square bowl in Altair Pattern.

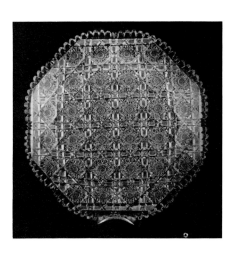

P 784. Maple City cut this 15-inch tray in the Temple Pattern.

C 786. Maple City signed this 8-inch bowl in the Crafton Pattern.

C 787. A 16 by 10-inch tray in Marswell Pattern signed Maple City.

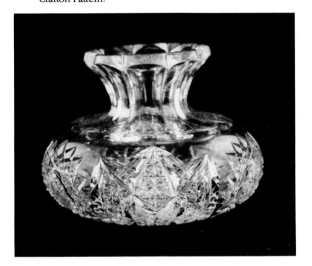

C 788. An 8-inch, tall flower center in Bonita Pattern, signed Maple City.

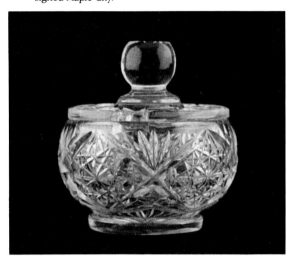

C 789. A mustard in Dodona Pattern by Maple City.

S 790. An 11-inch celery in Nirvana Pattern by Maple City.

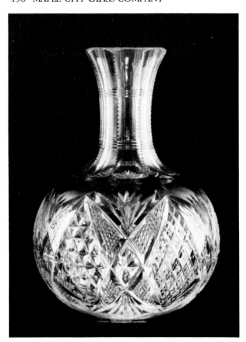

C 791. A 7-inch, tall carafe in Roma Pattern by Maple City.

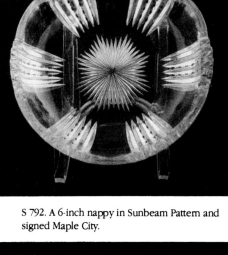

S 792. A 6-inch nappy in Sunbeam Pattern and signed Maple City.

C 793. An 8-inch, tall flower holder in Kenwood Pattern by Maple City.

C 794. Maple City signed this 11-inch vase.

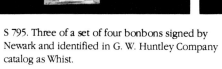

S 795. Three of a set of four bonbons signed by Newark and identified in G. W. Huntley Company catalog as Whist.

S 796. A 9-inch bowl in Whist Pattern by Newark.

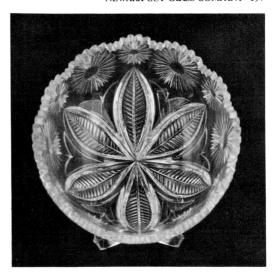

S 797. Parsche called the pattern on this 9-inch tray Aster.

NEWARK CUT GLASS COMPANY Newark, New Jersey 1906-1918

The company signed several pieces of glass, such as a set of four bonbons (S 795) with spade missing and a bowl (S 796). A G. W. Huntley Company catalog refers to the pattern as "Whist", a game that preceded bridge. A Parsche catalog called set in similar shapes euchre prizes, the name of another card game.

F. X. PARSCHE & SON COMPANY Chicago, Illinois 1876-1989

Frank X. Parsche immigrated from Bohemia but did not open his own cutting shop until 1876. On his death his son and then his grandson, Donald C. Parsche, carried on the glass cutting. Donald continues to repair cut glass at his home after he closed the shop.

Pointed Loops: Aster (S 797)
Dual Motifs: Cyrano (C 798)

QUAKER CITY CUT GLASS COMPAN Philadelphia, Pennsylvania 1902-1927

This company formed a part of the Cut Glass Corporation of America until 1907, then it took the name of Quaker City Cut Glass Company. A patent for a paper label showed the bust of William Penn. Copies of two published catalogs illustrate extensively cut patterns as well as some public domain ones with different names.

Bars: Comet (C 799), Walton (C 800).
Star: Rambler (P 801)
Dual Motifs: Coral (C 802), Fairview (C 803), Harvard (C 804), Lorraine (C 805), Venus (S 806)

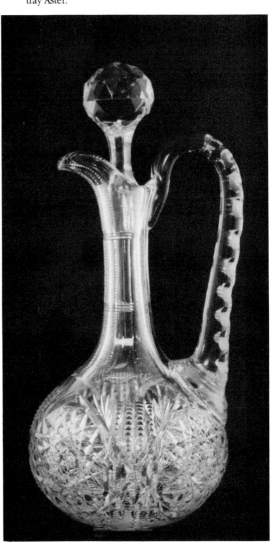

C 800. A 10-inch decanter in Walton Pattern by Quaker City.

C 798. An 8-inch bowl in Cyrano Pattern by Parsche.

C 799. A 10-inch, tall triangular decanter in Comet Pattern by Quaker City.

P 801. A star outline on this 10-inch tray in Rambler Pattern by Quaker City.

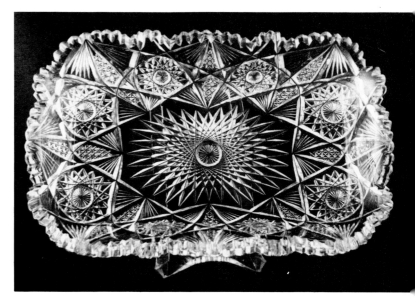

C 802. Quaker City cut the Coral Pattern on this 14 by 9-inch tray.

C 803. A 7.5-inch, tall comport in Fairview Pattern by Quaker City.

C 804. Quaker City called the pattern on this 12 by 8.5-inch tray Harvard.

C 805. A 10-inch celery in Lorraine by Quaker City.

S 806. Quaker City called this pattern on a whiskey tumbler Venus.

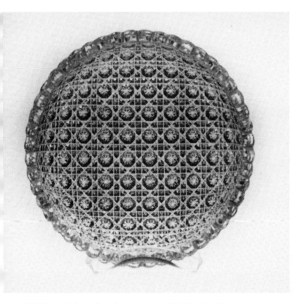

C 807. An 8-inch bowl in pattern #534 by Sterling.

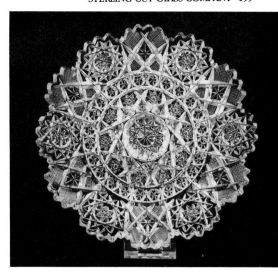

C 808. A 7-inch plate in pattern #592 by Sterling.

STERLING CUT GLASS COMPANY Cincinnati, Ohio ca. 1902-

The Sterling Cut Glass Company signed with a scripted name but identified most of the patterns with a number for each shape—even with the same pattern. The company went out of business in 1950, but the employees re-organized the firm. Two patterns appeared frequently in different collection and in one catalog: #534 (C 807) and #592 (C 808)

TAYLOR BROTHERS Philadelphia, Pennsylvania 1902-1915

A number of items produced by this company contained an acid-etched signature. Florence Vay, a daughter of one brother who founded the company, permitted the American Cut Glass Association to reprint a catalog. The company introduced the colonial edge seen on the Bellevue (P 809) and other patterns. Most patterns used a dual motifs outline: Crystal (P 810), Dawson #15 (S 811), Florence (S 812), Newton (P 813), Erma or #300 (S 814), #678 (C 815)

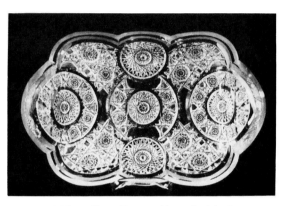

P 809. The Bellevue Pattern with a colonial edge on a tray, 12 by 8 inches, by Taylor Brothers.

S 811. A celery, 11.5 by 4 inches in Dawson #15 Pattern by Taylor Brothers.

P 810. A 7 by 8-inch, covered bonbon in Crystal Pattern by Taylor Brothers.

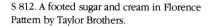

S 812. A footed sugar and cream in Florence Pattern by Taylor Brothers.

P 813. Taylor Brothers signed this compotier in Newton Pattern.

SILVER COMPANIES

Some cut glass companies hired others to add the decorative silver. Other companies added cutting shops. Eventually International Silver Company took over Meriden and Wilcox.

MERIDEN SILVER PLATE COMPANY Meriden, Connecticut 1895-1923

The Meriden Silver Plate Company added a cutting shop and did the fittings. Most collectors associate the company with the Alhambra Pattern or the flashed star motif, but the shop designed many diverse patterns, some it named and others it numbered.

1. GEOMETRICS

Bars: #126 (C 816), #324F (C 817)

Rows: PH&S (C 818)

Star: #796F (C 819)

Pointed Loops: #161 (P 820)

Dual Motifs: #246 (P 821), #258 (C 822), #891 (S 823)

2. FLORALS

Mayflower (S 824), #270 (S 825), #290 (S 826), #304 (C 827)

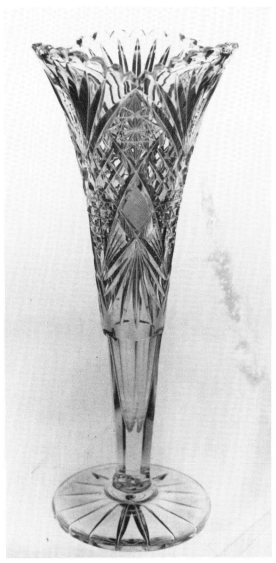

S 814. A 14-inch vase by Taylor Brothers in Erma Pattern or #300.

C 815. A 10-inch comport in pattern #678 by Taylor Brothers.

C 816. Meriden numbered the pattern on this 7-inch plate #126.

C 817. Meriden identified the pattern on this bonbon as #342F.

C 818. A tray, 10 by 8 inches, in pattern PH&S by Meriden. (4C substitute new print).

P 820. A 10-inch bowl in pattern #161 by Meriden.

C 819. A 12-inch tray in pattern #716F by Meriden.

P 821. A covered comport, 6 by 5 inches, in pattern #246 by Meriden.

C 822. An 11-inch vase in pattern #258 by Meriden.

S 824. A 9-inch plate in Mayflower by Meriden.

S 823. Meriden numbered this footed toothpick holder #891.

S 825. On a butter tub Meriden numbered the pattern #270.

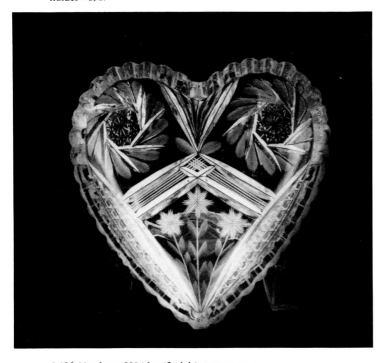

S 826. Number #290 identified this pattern on a bonbon by Meriden.

C 827. A handkerchief box in pattern #304 by Meriden.

S 829. A 10.5-inch plate in Excelsior Pattern by Wilcox.

WILCOX SILVER PLATE COMPANY Meriden, Connecticut 1865-1900
The company added a cutting shop and produced at least one catalog.
Border and Miter: Prism (S 828)
Star: Excelsior (S 829)
Pointed Loops: Utica (C 830)
Hallmark: tooth powder bottle (C 831), plate (C 832)

S 828. A 7-inch sauce bottle in Prism Pattern by Wilcox,

C 830. Wilcox called this pattern on a 9-inch, square bowl Utica.

C 832. The Wilcox hallmark appears on the silver of this 11-inch plate.

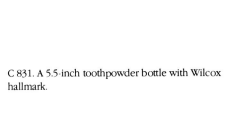

C 831. A 5.5-inch toothpowder bottle with Wilcox hallmark.

C 834. Unger called this pattern Sherwood, cut on this 10-inch, tall comport.

C 833. This 10-inch plate in the Beaumont Pattern appears in the Unger catalog.

UNGER BROTHERS Newark, New Jersey 1901-1918

This company added a cutting shop but still placed the main emphasis on silver. The company published two catalog combining the silver and the cut glass.

Bars: Beaumont (C 833)

Rows: Sherwood (C 834)

Gothic Arch: Arlington (C 835)

Pointed Loops: Arcadia (S 836), Fawn (C 837), Rosedale (C 838), signed saucer (C 839)

Circles: Circle (P 840), Regent (C 841)

Dual Motifs: Sandymount (P 842), Somerset (C 843), signed oil (S 844)

C 835. The pattern on this upright spoonholder Unger named Arlington.

S 836. A 6-inch plate in Arcadia Pattern by Unger.

C 837. A 12-inch, tall comport in Fawn Pattern by Unger.

C 839. A 4.5-inch saucer signed Unger.

C 838. Unger identified this pattern on a 10-inch plate as Rosedale.

P 840. An 8-inch bowl in Circle Pattern signed Unger.

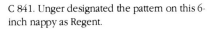

P 842. An 11-inch decanter in Sandymount by Unger.

C 841. Unger designated the pattern on this 6-inch nappy as Regent.

C 843. Unger named this pattern on a 10-inch decanter Somerset.

S 844. An oil signed Unger.

C 845. A 6-inch, tall comport in Argosy Pattern by Alford.

JEWELRY STORES AND SHOPS

A number of companies bought directly from the cutting shops or factories and sold in stores. Some of these published their own catalogs for mail orders, and two used an acid-etched signature.

C. G. ALFORD & COMPANY New York City 1872-1918

Alford operated a jewelry and watch repair shop. The following identifications came from a published catalog or a signature. The company cut two patterns in the dual motifs outline: Argosy (C 845) and Portland (C 846).

AVERBECK CUT GLASS COMPANY New York City 1892-1923

Averbeck maintained a retail jewelry store as well as conducted a large mail-order business in cut glass so they published a catalog. Often the catalog kept the pattern name given by the company that produced it, so you will find different patterns illustrated with the same name. The company used an acid signature of its own.

Border and Miter: Ruby (C 847)
Star: Saratoga (C 848)
Dual Motifs: Daisy (C 849), Frisco (S 850), Pricilla (S 851), Radium (C 852)

C 846. A 7-inch, tall carafe in Portland Pattern by Alford.

C 847. Averbeck called this 9-inch, tall cigar jar Ruby.

C 848. A 12-inch tray in Saratoga Pattern by Averbeck.

C 849. An 8-inch vase in Daisy Pattern and signed Averbeck.

S 850. Averbeck named this pattern on a 5-inch saucer Frisco.

C 852. A small cologne in Radium Pattern by Averbeck.

S 851. A 5-inch saucer in Pricilla Pattern by Averbeck.

C 853. A 14-inch tray in pattern #72015 by
Marshall Field.

C 854. Marshall Field identified this two-handled,
8-inch bowl as pattern #72037.

MARSHALL FIELD & COMPANY Chicago, Illinois

This department store hired different glass companies, such as Parsche and Fry, to create patterns. The patterns became the exclusive use of the department store. The catalogs numbered the patterns, and each shape in the same pattern received a different number. This panel pattern received the #72015 (C 853), and a pointed loops outline #72037 (C 8854)

PORCELAIN COMPANIES

Two companies originally began with sale of porcelain, then added a glass cutting shop at a later date. The following dates cover the cut glass period only.

C. F. MONROE Meriden, Connecticut 1903-1916

Art glass known aa Wavecrest highlighted the production of this company until it added a cutting shop. The company used Wavecrest shapes for the cutting blanks.
Bars: Olga (C 855
Border and Miter: Prism (C 856), Sylph (C 857)
Dual Motifs: #13 G. I. (C 858), #14 G. I. (C 859), #19 W. X (C 860)

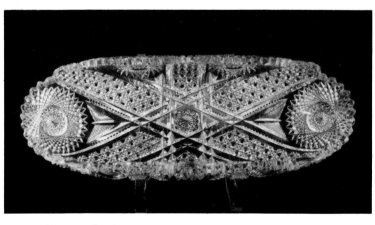

C 856. Monroe called the pattern on this jug
Prism.

C 857. An 8-inch bowl in Sulph Pattern by
Monroe.

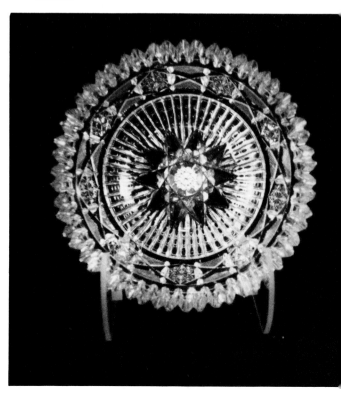

C 855. A 12-inch celery in bar outline by Monroe
in Olga Pattern.

C 858. Monroe identified this pattern on a 10-inch bowl as 13 G. I.

L. STRAUS & SONS New York City 1888-1917

Lazarus Straus immigrated from Bavaria and settled in Georgia where he worked for an art import company. He moved to New York and added cut glass to his import business. In 1917 the company patented the last cut glass pattern.

Bars: Americus (C 861), Electra (P 862), Granola (S 863)
Rows: Capri (S 864), patent #79806 (S 865)
Gothic Arch: Ducal (P 866), Fatima (C 867), Khedive (S 868)
Panels: Patent #38733 (S 869)
Pointed Loops: Corinthian (S 870)
Dual Motifs: Rosette (S871), signed underplate (S 872), signed celery (C 873)

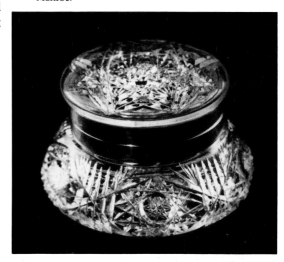

C 859. A jewel box in #14 G. I. Pattern by Monroe.

C 860. Monroe signed this 5-inch jewel box on the silver in pattern #19 W. X.

C 861. Straus signed this 10-inch, tall basket in the Americus Pattern.

S 863. An 11-inch celery in Granola Pattern by Straus.

P 862. This ice tub, 10.5 by 6.5 inches, in Electra Straus signed.

S 864. An oval fruit bowl, 9 by 7 inches, in Capri
Pattern by Straus.

S 865. This 9-inch bowl in a row outline
identified by patent #49806 Straus created.

P. 866. A 16-inch tray in Ducal Pattern and signed
Straus.

C 867. A footed, rose globe in Fatima Pattern by
Straus.

S 868. Straus named this pattern on a rose globe
Khedive.

S 869. Straus signed this 8-inch bowl identified by patent 28733.

S 870. The Corinthian Pattern decorated this square bowl by Straus.

S 871. The pattern on this jug Straus called Rosette.

S 872. Straus signed this 8-inch underplate for a vase.

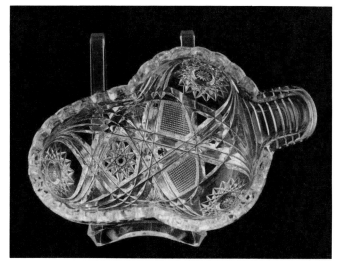

C 873. Straus signed this celery in an odd shape.

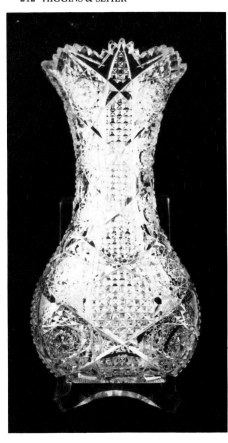

C 875. This vase in a bar outline Higgins & Seither identified as Mars.

C 874. A Higgins & Seiter catalog gave the name of the cheese cover and plate as Chyrsanthemum.

WHOLESELLERS

A number of companies bought from the factories and cutting shops, then sold at wholesale prices to stores and by mail order. The catalogs may use a number, the same name as that of the producer, or give the item a new name. The following list includes identified patterns by actual pieces.

HIGGINS & SEITER

This firm sold both china and cut glass. It produced catalogs showing only cut glass and others with a combination of cut glass and china. Patterns identified from catalogs include:

Bars: Chrysanthemum (C 874), Mars (C 875)
Rows: Brunswick (C 876)
Pointed Loops: Stella (C 877)
Dual Motifs: Crescent (C 878)

C 876. Higgins & Seiter catalog showed this horse-radish jar as Brunswick.

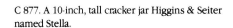

C 877. A 10-inch, tall cracker jar Higgins & Seiter named Stella.

C 878. A 5-inch, tall spoonholder in Crescent Pattern by Higgins & Seiter.

S 879. This 4-inch olive in Olympia Pattern went
to each subscriber to the magazine LADIES
WORLD according to F. B. Tinker catalog.

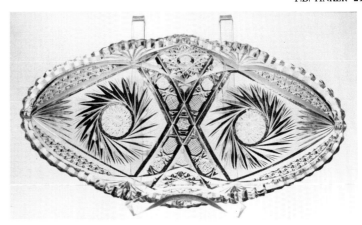

S 880. A Tinker catalog identified this 11-inch
celery as Abbott.

F. B. TINKER

This company operated out of Chicago. Two catalogs contained special sections
of cut glass by McCrea-Smith, Empire, and Fry. One catalog showed this olive dish in
Olympia (S 879) as a gift to anyone who subscribed to the magazine LADIES
WORLD.

Bars: Abbot (C 880)

Star: Dalton (S 881)

Gothic Arch: Star (C 882)

WALLENSTEIN MAYER COMPANY

This wholeseller numbered all patterns in the catalog. One pictures this tray in the
gothic arch outline #11721 (C 883) another in a circle outline #11808 (C 884).

S 881. A 9-inch, footed cake tray a Tinker catalog
called Dalton.

C 882. Tinker called this pattern on a 10-inch tray
Star.

C 883. Wallenstein Mayer & Company catalog
numbered this pattern #11721.

C 884. A 7-inch plate in pattern #11808 shown in Wallenstein Mayer catalog.

C 886. A Clapperton catalog showed this 8-inch bowl as Maple Leaf Pattern.

C 887. A 12-inch tray in Clover Pattern signed Clapperton.

C 885. This puff box signed Clapperton a catlog lists as Hob Pattern.

CANADIAN CUT GLASS

The Canadian companies used blanks from the United States and also from Europe. The blanks from Europe have a grayish tint caused by the chemical agent used to remove impurities from the metal. Most of patterns identified came from Grundy-Clapperton Company in Toronto. The Phillips Glass Company bought Grundy, Clapperton and still operates today.

Rows: Hob (C 885)

Gothic Arch: Maple Leaf (C 886)

Pointed Loops: Clover (C 887).

Dual Motifs: Classic (C 888), Cordelia (S 889), Norman (S 890), #756 (S 891), D (S 892).

Although Birks signed this bowl Clapperton identifies it in a catalog as Venice Star (C 893).

Any identification adds to the value of a piece of cut glass. Most collectors and dealers, however, give more value to identification of the original source rather than a secondary one, such as a wholeseller. In fact, identification from certain companies increases the value more than from others. But any identification of glass by a secondary source may eventually lead you to the original producer. So let research challenge you to learn more about your cut glass.

C 888. A whiskey jug and tumbler in Classic Pattern by Clapperton.

S 889. A 10-inch decanter in Cordelia Pattern by Clapperton.

S 890. A syrup in Norman Pattern by Clapperson.

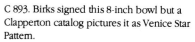

S 892. A Clapperton catalog designated this master salt "D".

C 893. Birks signed this 8-inch bowl but a Clapperton catalog pictures it as Venice Star Pattern.

S 891. Clapperton numbered the pattern #756 on this 10-inch comport.

Chapter 8
Questions and Some Answers

C 894. An 8-inch bowl in the simple Brazilian Pattern.

C 895. Hawkes signed this 10-inch jug in the Brazilian Pattern with the 8-point star, identical to that of Dorflinger.

In collecting cut glass you soon run into the problem of pattern duplication by various companies. By knowing who duplicated patterns and which ones offer some partial answers.

INFORMATION ON DUPLICATED PATTERNS

Different situations led to the duplication of patterns. A pattern designer took a position with another company or opened his own. He continued to cut the patterns he created for the other company. Companies did not patent all patterns, so anyone could copy them. A patent only lasted from seven to fourteen years, and then it went into public domain for anyone to copy. At times a company agreed to let another firm cut a certain pattern. These represent only a few explanations for duplication. As a collector or dealer you'll find these types of duplication.

1. Same Pattern, Same Name

Both Hawkes and Dorflinger produced two versions of the Brazilian Pattern: a simple one (C 894) and another with an 8-point star (C 895). Unless Hawkes signed the pieces, as he did on the jug, either company could have produced it.

2. Same Pattern, Different Name

When a company cut the same pattern of another firm, it usually changed the name.

Bars: (C 896) Empire Seneca and Pitkin & Brooks Athole (S 897); Clark Scotch, Hoare Signora, and signed Libbey; (S 898) Dorflinger #50 and Hoare Acme.

Rows: (S 899) Dorflinger Hob Diamond, Hawkes Hobnail, Mt. Washington Hexagon Diamond (C 900), Empire Royal, Pairpoint Two-Cut Octagon, Clapperton Hob Star, Roden Queenton (S 901) Dorlinger #28, Mt. Washington Wheeler, Wilcox Waldorf

Border and Miter: (S 902) Bergen Florida, Dorflinger unnamed, Pairpoint Cambridge, Sinclaire signed

Star: (S 903) Alford Tokio, Empire Century, Fry Sunbeam, Quaker City Venus; (S 904), Empire Nelson, Hawkes Dundee, Pitkin & Brooks Nellore, Quaker City Rosewood

Panels: (C 905) Hoare Monarch, Unger Cornell

Pointed Loops: (C 906) Laurel Vittoria, Parsche Laurel Wreath

Dual Motifs: (S 907) Bergen Flake, Elmira #6; (S 908) Alford Verona, Clark Galatea; (S 909) Clark AU, signed Alford; (S 910) Bergen Velma, Fry Almond; (C 911) Fry Wreath, Hoare #7757; (C 912) Hawkes Palermo, Quaker City Gem; (C 913) Blackmere Almont, Clark Harvard, Quaker City Melrose, Taylor Brothers #2; (C 914) Irving Juliette, Libbey Gloria; (C 915) Libbey Venetia, Roden Newton; (S 916) Averbeck Lowell, Pitkin & Brooks Sulton; (S 917) Pairpoint Gretna, Unger Andover; (C 918) Higgins & Seiter Webster, signed Almy & Thomas, signed Straus

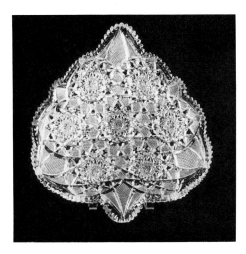

C 896. A 13 by 12 inch tray in Athole Pattern by Pitkin and Brooks or Seneca by Empire.

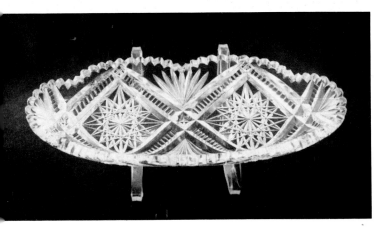

S 897. An 11.5-inch celery in Scotch Pattern by
Clark, Signora by Hoare, and signed by Libbey.

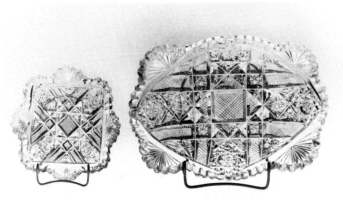

S 898. Dorflinger number this pattern in a butter
set #50, but Hoare called it Acme.

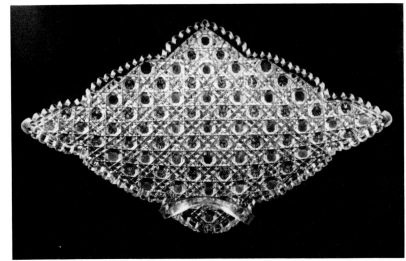

C 900. A 17 by 10 inch tray in Royal Pattern by
Empire, 2 Cut Octagon by Pairpoint, Hob Star by
Clapperton, and Queenton by Roden.

S 902. A carafe in Florida Pattern by Bergen,
Cambridge by Pairpoint, unnamed by Dorflinger,
and signed by Sinclaire.

S 899. A jug in Hob Diamond Pattern by
Dorflinger, Hobnail by Hawkes, or Hexagon
Diamond by Mt. Washington.

S 901. A 7-inch plate in #28 Pattern by Dorflinger,
Wheeler by Mt. Washington, and Waldorf by
Wilcox.

S 903. A 6-inch, crimped bowl in Tokio Pattern by Alford, Century by Empire, Sunbeam by Fry, and Venus by Quaker City.

S 904. An 11.5-inch celery in Nelson Pattern by Empire, Dundee by Hawkes, Nellore by Pitkin & Brooks, Rosewood by Quaker City, and signed Fry.

S 905. Hoare called this 12-inch vase Monarch Pattern but Unger named it Cornell.

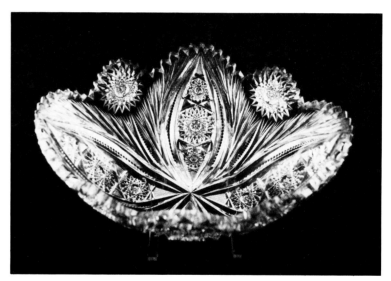

C 906. A 12-inch, oval fruit bowl in Vittoria Pattern by Laurel and Laurel Wreath by Parsche.

S 907. A 7-inch nappy in Flake Pattern by Bergen and #6 by Elmira.

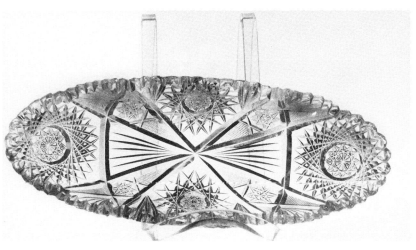

S 908. An 11-inch celery in Verona Pattern by Alford and Galatea by Clark.

S 909. Clark called this 7.5-inch plate A U Pattern, and Alford signed it.

C 910. Bergen name the pattern on the butter pat Velma, but Fry listed it as Almond.

C 912. This whiskey tumbler Hawkes call Palermo Pattern but Quaker City named it Gem.

C 911. Fry named the pattern on the tumblers Wreath, but Hoare numbered it #757.

C 913. An 8-inch bowl in Almont Pattern by Blackmer, Harvard by Clark, Melrose by Quaker City, #2 by Taylor Brothers.

C 914. The pattern on this 7-inch plate Libbey called Gloria while Irving cut it as Juliette.

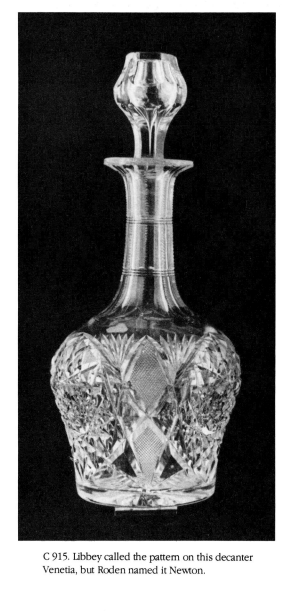

C 915. Libbey called the pattern on this decanter Venetia, but Roden named it Newton.

S 916. The pattern on this 7-inch plate Averbeck named Lowell, but Pitkin & Brooks called it Sultan.

S 917. A 5-inch saucer in Gretna by Pairpoint or Andover by Unger.

C 918. Almy & Thomas and Straus signed this 10-inch bowl, but Higgins & Seiter called the pattern Western.

S 919 Bergen substituted a pinwheel for a hobstar in in the Brighton Pattern cut on this 11-inch celery.

C 920. A 10-inch, low bowl in Troy Pattern by Fry with pinwheel rather than hobstar.

3. Change of Major Motif

When an Empire catalog showed a pattern with a hobstar but a collector owned the same one with a pinwheel, Bill Iorio, who worked for Empire, explained, "Any customer who placed a large order could have a hobstar changed to a pinwheel. The name of the game was to sell."

Catalogs from different companies showed the following patterns with a hobstar, but someone substituted a pinwheel for the major motif.

Bars: (S 919) Bergen Brighton

Circles: (C 920) Fry Troy, (C 921) Clark Crown

Dual Motifs: (C 922) Maple City Baltic, (S 923) Pitkin & Brooks Venice

Company catalogs pictured these patterns with a pinwheel, but actual pieces contained a hobstar.

S 921. An 8.5-inch jug signed Clark in the Crown Pattern but with a pinwheel rather than a hobstar.

C 922. A jug, 7.5-inch tall, in Baltic with a pinwheel and signed Maple City.

S 923. A 6-inch, tall carafe in Venice by Pitkin & Brooks but with a pinwheel and not a hobstar.

C 924. The Aurora Pattern shown in Higgins & Seiter catalog but with a pinwheel.

P 925. Dorflinger named the pattern Sonoma with a pinwheel.

Bars: (C 924) Higgins & Seiter Aurora
Gothic Arch: (P 925) Dorflinger Sonoma and (P 926) with hobstars.
Dual Motifs: (P 927) Alford Florence, (C 928) Egginton Atlas
These patterns illustrated changes in other dominate motifs by various companies.
Bars: (C 929) Hoare #1564 hobstar for flashed star
Dual Motifs: (C 930) Meriden #194 original, (C 931) same pattern but with a flashed star, (P 932) original pattern Cut Star on a Matt Background used a 5-point star, but this has a hobstar. (P 933) Hoare named a pattern Cob Web with squares of crosscut diamonds, but he changed the pattern to #5429 that contained squares of cane, otherwise identical.

P 926. The same pattern as Sonoma except with a hobstar.

P 927. An Alford catalog pictured this pattern as Florence but with a pinwheel.

C 928. The Egginton catalog showed this pattern as Atlas with a pinwheel, but this 9-inch bowl has a hobstar.

C 929. A 10-inch bowl in pattern #1564, signed Hoare, but with a hobstar and not a flashed one.

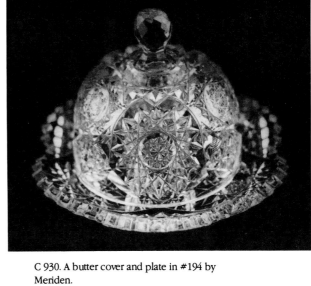

C 930. A butter cover and plate in #194 by Meriden.

P 933. Hoare cut the Spider Web Pattern with squares of crosscut diamonds, but on pattern #5934 the company merely substituted cane in the squares on the 14-inch, signed tray.

P 932. Dorflinger produced this pattern of Cut Star on a Matt Background with a 5-point star, but this piece has hobstars. David Dorflinger identified it as cut by Dorflinger.

C 931. A 14-inch decanter in #194 by Meriden but with a flashed star.

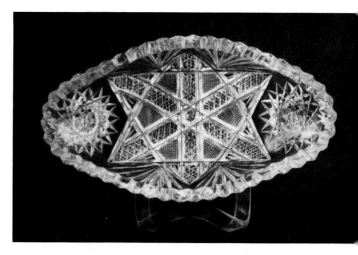

P 935. Libbey signed a relish dish but put crosscut diamonds on the bars and substituted crosshatching for fans.

S 934. Quaker City called the pattern with crosshatched bars on this 7-inch relish Heron.

4. Minor Motifs Changes

Unless you observe very carefully you may not note these minute changes on the minor motifs. Companies used such changes to break the patent.

Bars: (S 934) Quaker City crosshatched the bars, (S 935) a piece signed Libbey used the crosscut diamond on the bars, but Bergen's Argo cut the bars with crosshatching and star. (P 936) Hoare cut the original, curved bars with cane on one and notched miters on the other, for the Crystal City Pattern. On a ewer (P 937) signed Hoare he substituted intersecting miters for the cane.

Pointed Loops and Circles: (P 938) Averbeck Azalia, Bergen Claremont with crosshatching on loops; (P 939) Fry Duquesne, Quaker City Bellevue with nailhead diamond; Empire Climax with cane.

Pointed Loops and Bars: (P 940) Fry Chicago with cane; Bergen Oriole with crosshatching and stars; Laurel Glencoe with alternating crosshatching and nailhead diamond; Quaker City Lynhurst with alternating flat star and nailhead diamond.

P 936. In the original Crystal City Pattern, Hoare cut cane on one circling bar and notched miters on the overlapping one.

P 938. In this 14-inch tray Averbeck in Azalia Pattern and Bergen in Claremont crosshatched the loops.

P 937. On this ewer in Crystal City Pattern and signed, Hoare substituted intersecting, short miters for cane.

P 939. An 8-inch tray in Bellevue Pattern by Bergen, Climax by Empire, and Duquesne by Fry used nailheads on the loops.

5. Changes in Basic Patterns

Some companies developed several patterns from a basic outline. By changing the motifs that completed the outline, a new pattern resulted.

Bars: (C 941) By changing the decoration on the bar, Hoare created a new pattern named #1614, feathering the bar produced the Naples Pattern.

Border and Miter: Hoare changed the motifs on the border or used a different arrangement on miters for Hindoo, Pluto, and Haydn (See Chapter 6 under Hoare.) (P 942) A Hoare catalog showed curved miters on the Croesus Pattern, but the decanter signed Hoare (P 943) has straight ones.

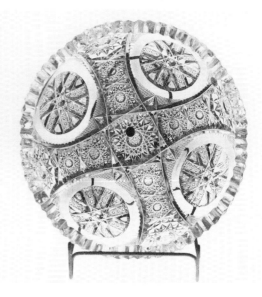

P 940. Four companies produced this pattern with slight differences in the minor motifs on the intersecting bars in the circles: Oriole by Bergen with crosshatching and star, Chicago by Fry with caned bars, Glencoe by Laurel with nailhead and crosshatched motifs, and Lynhurst by Quaker City which alternated nailhead and flat stars.

C 941. Hoare crosshatched the bars on this 8-inch bowl in #1614, feathered them for the Naples Pattern.

P 942. In the Croesus Pattern Hoare curved the miters.

P 943. In this 6-inch decanter signed Hoare, the company duplicated the Croesus Pattern but substituted straight miters

C 944. Libbey outlined the pattern on this 10-inch tray in Colonna Pattern with a star and filled in with hobstars.

C 945. On this 7-inch plate in Waverly Pattern, Libbey cut a 5-point star in the center of the combinaion motif.

Star: Libbey created at least three patterns from this star arrangement: Colonna (C 944), Waverly (C 945), an unidentified one signed Libbey (C 946).

Panels: Hawkes created several patterns based on the panel outline (See Chapter 6 under Hawkes).

Dual Motifs: Clark used a basic outline to create several patterns. By substituting a hobstar or pinwheel as the major motif or changing the bottom motif of the combination, he created a new pattern (See Chapter 6 under Clark).

Hawkes also created several patterns from a basic outline. By changing the major motif or alternating two or by substituting a crosshatched diamond for a fan, he created a new pattern (See Chapter 6 under Hawkes). A question arises as to the identification of this tray (P 947) cut in the Gladys Pattern by Hawke or Marlboro by Dorflinger as the upper fan turns down rather than up.

C 946. Libbey repeated the star outline on this 10-inch, signed bowl but sutstitute Russian where other two used stars.

C 947. This tray, 16 by 10 inches, duplicates the Gladys Pattern by Hawkes or Marlboro one by Dorflinger except for the reversed fan on the border.

C 948. This swirl pattern collectors found in different pieces signed by either Tuthill or Laurel.

S 949. Hawkes signed this olive dish, and a collector found the same pattern signed by Maple City.

6. Unexplained Oddities

You may discover that different companies signed different pieces in the same pattern. This happened when an agent sold the piece and used its signature. If two cutting shops sign the pieces, perhaps the patent had expired. Both Laurel and Tuthill signed this swirl pattern (C 948). Both Hawkes and Maple City signed this pattern on a nut bowl (S 949).

One company used the same pattern on two jugs but indicated the functions by the lids. The cracker jar (C 950) has a clear neck and flat lid while that of the tobacco one (P 951) fits tightly over the rim.

Different shapes caused a company to alter the pattern. A tray signed Pitkin & Brooks in King George (C 952) has an ornate border, but a cologne bottle shown in a catalog has none.

On January 15, 1901, Libbey received patents on two patterns: #33,909 and 33,910 for Sultana. In 33,909 the star points have crosshatching (C 953), but Sultana has crosscut squares.

The more glass you see and buy, the more duplications and oddities you will discover. In fact, the more you study patterns, the more questions arise, some you can answer and others you can't.

P 950. A cracker jar with a clear neck and flat, gold washed silver lid.

C 952. A 12-inch tray in King George Pattern signed by Pitkin & Brooks except the catalog showed no border on cologne or decanter.

P 951. The same pattern in a tobacco jar with a tight fitting, silver lid.

C 953. Libbey received a patent for two patterns on the same date with very little difference. Sultana used several squares on the star points, but patent #33,909 covered the points with crosshatching.

L 954. The Fry punch bowl in the Rochester
Pattern.

L 955. The "Astor" punch bowl.

WHATEVER HAPPENED TO?

As you read books and articles on cut glass and talk with knowledgeable dealers and collectors. you learn about the fabulous pieces featured at expositions or created for a wealthy client. Some have found a home in a museum. At the Toledo Museum of Art you can view the table, 32 inches tall and top 28 inches in diameter, in the Neola pattern and cut for the St. Louis Exposition in 1904. The Museum also houses the 24-inch punch bowl cut by John Rufus Denman for the same exposition. A collector owns the duplicate of the McKinley punch bowl. The original disappear from the White House after the assination of McKinley.

A little research supplied information on the following items.

1. Fry Punch Bowl

In 1905, at the Lewis and Clark Exposition in Portland, Oregon, Fry won the grand medal of honor award for a punch bowl in the Rochester Pattern. The bowl, 4½ feet tall and weighing 150 pounds contained 12 footed punch cups (L 954).

The punch bowl and table consisted of 6 distinct parts. Each part fit tightly into the one above. Most important each part functioned as a separate piece: the base became a flower center, the rounded piece a rose globe, the stem a vase, a tray, a stand for the 18-inch punch bowl or a comport.

At different times it went on display at the Carnegie Museum, Corning Museum, and even Disneyland. A collector now owns it.

2. Astor Punch Bowl

Hawkes cut this 24-inch punch bowl with 18 matching cups—all signed—for the Paris Exposition. The gothic outline resembles that of the Chyrsanthemum Pattern. Gorham put 110 ounces of silver in the rim (L 955).

In 1912, John Jacob Astor IV selected this punch set as a gift for his bride. He scheduled delivery after they returned from a honeymoon in Egypt. They returned on the Titantic. He perished, but she survived. In her grief she could not bring herself to accept the set. Several years later a wealthy banker and jewelry store owner purchased it and kept it for 50 years. A collector now owns it.

3. Ellsmere Banquet Lamp

Libbey cut two of these 35-inch, Ellsmere lamps for the 1893 Columbian Exposition (L 956). The lamp has the original chimney, and all pieces contain the Libbey signature, according to the owner and collector.

L 956. One of two lamps in the Ellsmere Pattern cut for the 1893 Exposition by Libbey.

L 957. The Hershey Torchere.

L 958. The lamp bought at the St. Louis Exposition.

4. The Hershey Glass Torchere

Mr. Milton Hershey purchased the torchere when he visited the Chicago World's Fair in 1893. The 12-foot torchere stands on a heavy steel base about three feet in diameter. Silver-coated sleeves cover the supporting column that contains the electrical wiring. The glass base consists of 12 pie-shaped pieces with numbers that form a circular structure. Cut and engraved collars decorate the column.

In the upper portion glass arms fit 30 lights in a network of crystal fleur-de-lis pendants and beads. A number of smaller branches and a finial complete the 1200 pieces that form the torchere. It weights 800 pounds (L 957).

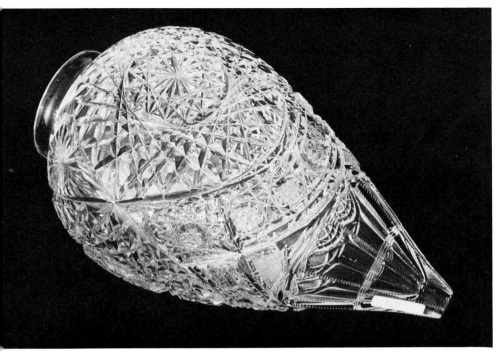

L 959. An enlarged view of one globe.

L 960. A candelabra once owned by Liberace.

Straus sold the torchere to Hershey, but a later theory suggested the Baccarat Company of France shipped the torchere to Straus in the form of press blanks. Straus cut the blanks and put the pieces together.

From 1901 to 1904 the torchere occupied the showroom of the Hershey soda shop, and next it went to the new Hershey home in 1908. In 1950, Hershey exhibited it in the Hershey Museum. Corning Museum put it on exhibit in 1977. At present the Milton S. Hershey School who owns the torchere has loaned it to the Hershey Museum of American Life. In taking the torchere apart, the person assigned to the job found a number of signatures on the metal base. No one knows whether they belong to Baccarat or the various craftsmen who have worked on the torchere.

5. Lamp From the St. Louis Exposition, 1904

Only Libbey and Quaker City exhibited at the St. Louis Exposition. This floor lamp or electrolier displayed by Quaker City measured 9 feet 3 inches. It has 21 globes and 532 prisms (L 958 & L 959). Its restoration required 9 months of work.

The present owner and collector has tried to identify the pattern and trace the history of ownership. Sam Meyer, owner of a store in Meriden, Mississippi, went to the St. Louis Fair and purchased it. The collector has talked to various members of the family, and one had a picture of herself with the lamp.

6. Hawkes Floor Lamp

The Lightner Museum displays a floor lamp presented by Hawkes to Henry W. Flagler, a close friend and collector. The lamp measures 6 feet 8 inches in height. The Hawkes cut glass catalog identifies it as "Golden Flame Amber" (See color section). Mr. Flagler founded the Lightner Museum.

7. Liberace Candelabra and Lamp

Liberace, in a way, made history of a sort with a candelabra. This candelabra did not sit on the piano while he performed, but it sold at the Liberace Collection Sale. It has four silver branches and 5 candles. The silver has a Meriden hallmark (L 960).

This 30-inch lamp adorned a crystal table in Liberace's penthouse. It contains a mushroom done, 4 hanging globes, 100 prisms, and six lights. No one has positively identified the lamp as cut by Quaker City (L 961), but the Lightner Museum has a duplicate of this lamp. The collector also purchased the lamp at the Liberace Collection Sale.

By no means does this represent a complete list of famous pieces, but let it stimulate you to look for more. You can easily recognize these fabulous piece because they represent quality-cut glass.

L 961. A lamp once owned by Liberace.

Chapter 9
Checklist for Quality

S 963. A small orange bowl in a standard category.

Quality in cut glass consists of a combination of special features that makes one piece worth more than another (P 962). To help you recognize the differences in qualities and to make our value guide easier to use, we have divided cut glass pieces picture in this book into four categories: standard, choice, premium, and limited.

To review a standard piece has a simple pattern but on a clear blank with an ordinary shape (S 963). A choice piece adds one or more quality features to these basic ones, such as an ornate pattern on a large shape, to make it more desirable (C 964). The premium classification combines a number of plus qualities—pattern, shape, sharpness, and polish—to make it outstanding (P 965).

Some museum-type pieces, however, defy classification as no one can give them a positive value but rather only what the buyer will pay. Consequently, we have placed them in a limited category (L 966).

Before each caption number for a picture, we have placed an S, C, P, or L. To use the value guide you check the shape under the quality indicated by the letter to secure the price range.

In setting up these quality categories we have studied the special features of each category and applied them to each piece of cut glass pictured. The following suggestions will guide you in recognizing these individual qualities in cut glass.

P 962. A 16 by 9-inch tray of high quality.

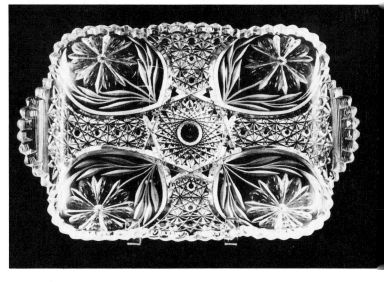

C 964. An 18 by 10-inch tray with handles in a Russian and floral pattern that rates the choice category.

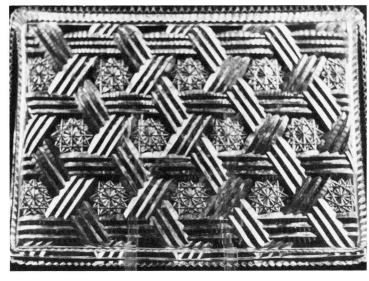

P 965. Quality in this 13 by 9-inch tray emphasizes the pattern.

PRIMARY QUALITIES

Any checking for quality begins with the type of pattern and the shape. The quality of either of these depends upon certain characteristics.

1. Pattern

To review, a pattern consists of a miter outline and the elaborating motifs. The combination of outline and motifs provides the quality of a pattern. Some collectors prefer the simple outlines as the bar (C 967) or row. Others favor the more ornate one, such as pointed loops or gothic arch (P 968). The deciding factors depend on the complexity and accuracy of cutting (C 969). This includes spacing of the outline and balance with other motifs. Both the dominant and minor motifs must blend with the miter outline and with each other (P 970).

The type of major motif can indicated quality. A hobstar (C 971) and a pinwheel required about the same amount of cutting. The more points on a star or swirls on a pinwheel, the higher the quality. The flashed star (S 972) or shooting star, by comparison, shows less quality and time required to cut.

The type of minor motifs improves the quality. Cane or small stars rate higher than crosshatching. Minor motifs often combine to form a single one (S 973). The combination must balance with the miter outline and with each other. The number of such combination must equal those of the major motifs.

The deep and detailed cutting of a pattern creates sharpness you can feel. The sharper the cutting, the greater the quality. The even sparkle of a piece of cut glass results from a combined acid and hand polish—acid for details and hand for large motifs (C 974).

L 966. This 15-inch coffee pot illustrates the limited category.

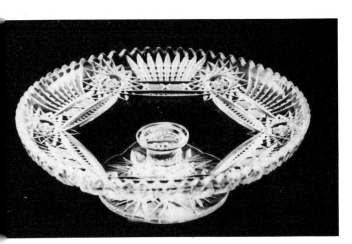

C 967. A well-balanced pattern signed Pitkin & Brooks in a footed cake tray.

P 968. A 9-inch, crimped, low bowl in gothic arch pattern.

C 969. A 7-inch plate shows balance in motifs.

P 970. A tray, 16 by 9 inches, emphasizes balance between major and minor motifs.

C 971. A 9-inch dish that focuses on hobstars as a dominant quality.

S 972. This 8-inch bowl features a flashed star as a dominate motif of lesser importance.

S 973. The combination motif in this plate balances with the major hobstar one.

C 974. A flower center that shows an excellent polish.

C 975. A 7-inch, square bowl in a combination star and pointed loops outline.

P 976. A 10-inch bowl with a deeply crimped rim.

2. Shape

Any deviation in shape from the regular form indicates quality. Companies changed the round shape of a bowl to square (C 975), six-sided, or crimped (P 976). A clear divider added another plus quality (C 977).

These changes in shapes carried over to trays. The following shapes competed with the oral tray: triangular (P 978), six sided (P 979), crimped (P 980), or a combined triangle and circle (P 981).

The rims on cut glass pieces suggest quality. Companies soon replaced the regular scallops with alternating large and small ones. A step cutting on a scalloped rim raised the quality even more.

Small pieces offer choices in quality shapes. In a sugar and cream look for an odd shape (C 982), a set with a foot, low or tall (C 983), or double lips (C 984). No handles on a set can rate higher than some with handles. Bonbons offer a variety of choices in shapes (P 985).

The shape of most lidded pieces rank as quality. Such pieces include: a 3-piece ice bowl (P 986), a bedroom set (C 987), tobacco jar (C 988), cracker jar (C 989), and this rounded jar (P 990). A mushroom set, some with silver divider, (P 991) or a jewel box (C 992) contain extra qualities.

Most companies did not produce special shapes in large numbers, so the scarcity increases the value. Consider these examples: cornucopia (P 993), decanter with a controlled top (P 994), handled mug (P 995), canned milk holder (P 996), or desk lamp (P 997). In this group should come clocks. Sinclaire, Pairpoint, Hawkes, Libbey (P 998), and an unknown company (P 999) produced small clocks.

C 977. A 7-inch, divided bowl with two handles.

P 978. A 9-inch tray shaped as a triangle.

P 979. A six-sided tray cut in decorative bars.

P 980. A 12-inch tray with a crimped shape.

P 981. A 12-inch tray in a combined shape of round and triangular.

C 982. An unusual shape in a sugar and cream by Dorflinger in the Celtic Pattern.

C 983. A footed cream to a set has a unique shape and decorated handle.

C 984. A cream with two handles and two lips.

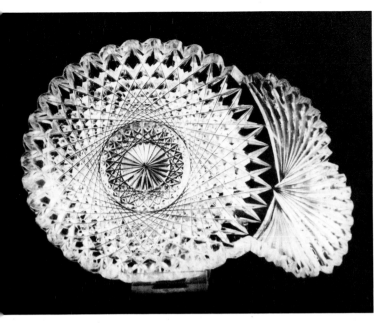

C 985. An 8-inch bonbon with a fan-cut handle.

P 986. A three-part, ice bowl with liner and lid.

C 987. A bedroom set adds a spout, handle, and top to a carafe shape.

C 988. The shape and pattern of this tobacco jar indicates its quality.

C 989. A cracker jar, 11.5 by 8.5 inches, shows quality in pattern, shape, and size.

P 990. The shape of this covered jar blends perfectly with the pattern.

P 991. A mushroom set in pattern #136 by Meriden has an ice liner in silver.

C 992. The hinged jewel box has an 8-sided shape that adds quality.

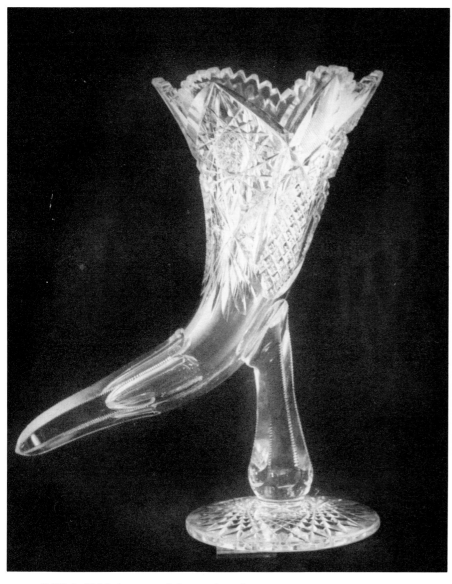

P 993. An 11.5-inch cornucopia has scarcity and shape as dominant qualities.

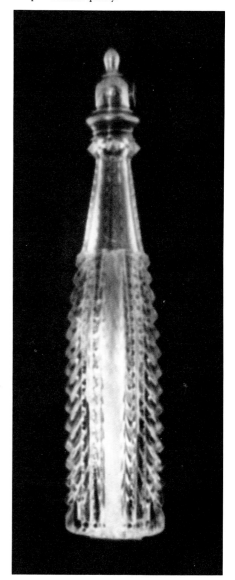

P 994. This decanter, 14.5 inches, contains a controlled top that pours one drink at a time.

P 995. This 6-inch mug has a base, decorated handle, and balanced pattern.

P 996. This container for canned milk has a hole in the bottom of the holder to push the can out.

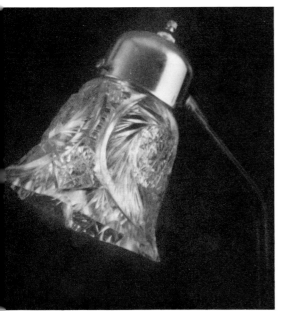

P 997. A desk lamp with silver fittings.

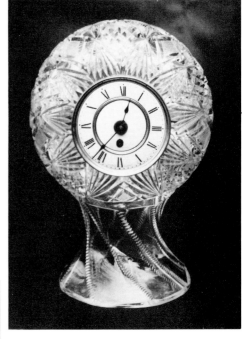

P 998. An unusual shape for a clock in Harvard Pattern by Libbey.

P 999. Another clock in the regular shape used by most companies.

C 1000. This syrup has a scolloped base and an upturned lip to prevent drips.

C 1001. A syrup with a base and silver lid and handle.

C 1002. An 8-inch bowl with an added base.

EXTRA FEATURES

Companies use basic shapes for various pieces of cut glass. Whenever a company added another feature to a regular shape, the quality increased. Such additions require more work and increased the cost of production. A base formed one of the most popular additions

1. Base

A base refers to a round or scolloped, disc-like shape attached to a piece of cut glass. Under the base, the craftsman cut a star or combination motif as cane. The shape, type of star, or combination motif determine the quality. Companies added a base to a topless syrup (C 1000), a silver topped syrup (C 1001), a bowl (C 1002), or a jug (C 1003). Most considered a base as the regular part of a comport (S 1004).

C 1003. A 12-inch jug with a base and decorated handle.

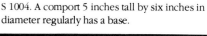

S 1004. A comport 5 inches tall by six inches in diameter regularly has a base.

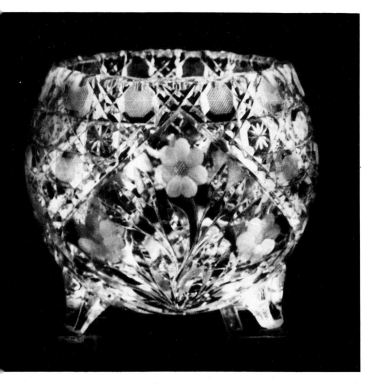

S 1005. A rose globe with peg feet.

2. Foot

A foot consists of three types: peg, low, and tall. A fern contained peg feet as a regular feature. When the company added peg feet to a rose globe (S 1005), an urn (P 1006), a covered bonbon (P 1007), or a small bonbon (C 1008) the value increased. The addition of crosshatching or a star under the foot raised the value.

A low and tall foot combined a base with a stem. The two types differed only in the height of the stem. Companies shaped the stem round, fluted, or square and added notching and even engraved flowers. A low foot increased the quality of these pieces: a jug (C 1009), a wine jug (P 1010), a low bowl (P 1011), orange bowl (P 1012).

A round knob can substitute for a stem (C 1013). A two-part, punch bowl usually has a conical foot. The addition to this conical base of a stem, knob, and collar greatly raises the quality (P 1014)

A tall stem adds more quality to a piece of cut glass than a short one (C 1015). The difference in quality between two, tall-stemmed piece depends on the decoration on the stem and under the base (C 1016). Any deviation in the shape of a stem (C 1017) or in the decoration commands a higher value. In this footed bowl, the scolloped hobstar on the base, and the decorated stem develop the quality (C 1018). In a two-part, cake tray the hobstar base, the bulge in the stem for a teardrop, and the decorated collar earned a limited rating, (L 1019).

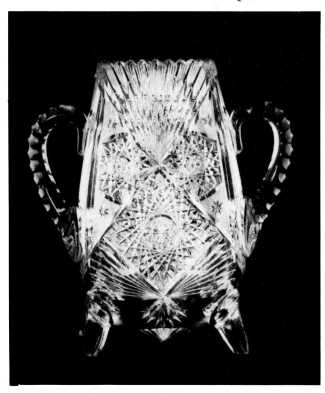

P 1006. A 12-inch urn with peg feet and decorated, vertical handles.

C 1008. A 7-inch bonbon with peg feet.

P 1007. A covered bonbon, 9.5 by 7.5, with curled, peg feet.

C 1009. A jug with a low foot, punty-cut handle, and hobnails pattern cut under the base.

P 1011. An 8-inch, low bowl in a detailed pattern on a low foot.

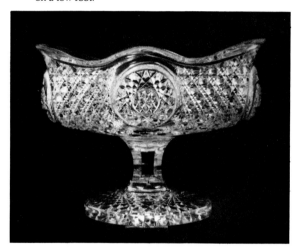

P 1012. A 9-inch, orange bowl with a low foot, heavily cut pattern, and scolloped rim.

P 1010. A 13.5-inch, wine jug with heavily cut handles and low foot.

C 1013. A 3.5-inch toothpick holder with a clear knob substituted for a short stem.

P 1014. An ornate punch bowl, 12 by 12 inches, with a a bulbous stem and decorated collar.

C 1015. The plus qualities on this 11.5-inch celery include pattern, tall foot, and paneled stem.

C 1016. A 12-inch celery with a detailed pattern, notched panel stem and hobstar cut under the foot.

C 1017. A 12-inch orange bowl with clear panels topping the notched ones in the rest of the tall stem.

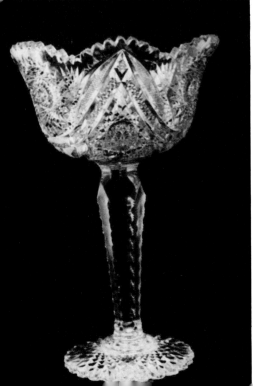

C 1018. A footed bowl, 11 by 7 inches, in gothic arch pattern, punty-decorated stem, and scolloped base cut with a hobstar.

L 1019. This two-part, cake tray received a limited rating because of the size, 12.5 by 9.5 inches, the detailed pattern, a stem with a collar and bulbous shape for a teardrop, and a hobstar cut under the foot.

P 1020. A tray, 14 by 9 inches, has handles blown into the blank.

C 1021. An 8-inch relish signed Hawkes with two applied handles.

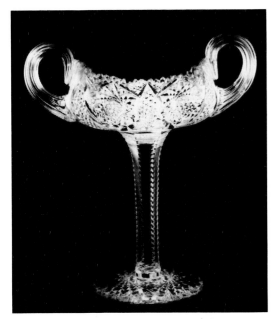

C 1022. A 10-inch comport with two, miter-cut handles.

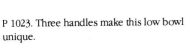

P 1023. Three handles make this low bowl unique.

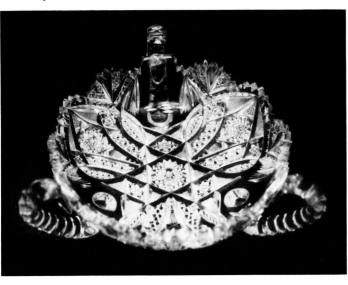

3. Handles

When the blower included a space for a handle on a blank as in this tray (P 1020) or in an ice tub, the shape received little increase in quality. The quality increases on this two-handled relish signed Hawkes as the regular shape did not have handles (C 1021). Two handles added to the regular shape of a comport raised the value (C 1022). A low bowl with three handles triples the quality (P 1023).

Check the position of applied handles on an ice bowl. Horizontal handles (P 1024) add more quality than vertical ones (C 1025). The position of the handles on an urn (P 1026) or a wine decanter (P 1027) upgrade the quality.

P 1024. An ice bowl, 14.5 by 9.5 inches, signed Hoare, has honeycombed, horizontal handles.

C 1025. An ice bowl with vertical handles decorated with stars and fans.

In addition to the placement of handles study the decorations. The previous examples have single thumbprints, honeycomb, parallel miters, rings, or stars and fans. The last motifs add the most quality.

4. Necks

Necks received special treatment, too. Libbey introduced the bulging neck on decanters, and Dorflinger and others favored neck rings. Notched flutes (C 1028) added little, step cut slightly increases the quality (P 1029), and honeycomb rated at the top ((1030).

P 1026. Two, highly placed handles on this urn adds an extra quality.

C 1028. This 8.5-inch carafe has notched panels on the neck.

P 1027. The placement of the handle on this 14-inch, wine decanter provides a plus quality.

C 1029. A 12-inch whiskey decanter in Royal Pattern by Hunt has a step-cut neck.

P 1030. An 8-inch carafe in Meriden pattern #208 contains a honeycomb neck.

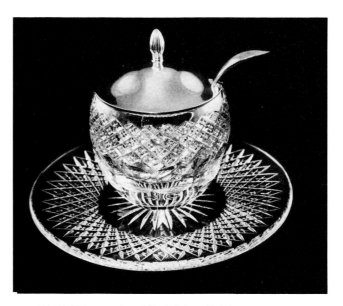

C 1031. This one-piece, jelly dish has a little less quality than that of a two-piece one.

5. Underplates

Attached under plates (C 1031) do not offer the quality of a separate one (C 1032). A deep underplate with a decorated border for covered butter or cheese (P 1033) indicates quality. Increase the value of a cracker jar with a scolloped underplate (P 1034).

These suggestions on quality features provide you with a starting point to make your own checklist.

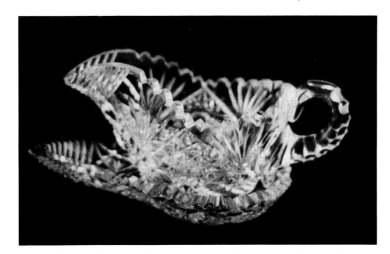

C 1032. Two pieces increase the quality of this oval, sauce dish.

P 1034. A cracker jar in Russian Pattern with a scolloped underplate.

P 1033. The deep, underplate for this covered butter and the pattern provide the extra qualities.

L 1036. A 13-inch, patriotic plate illustrates a
novelty.

TREASURE HUNTING

While you concentrate on adding quality cut glass to your collection, treasure
hunt for additional enhancements. Awareness of them often prompts you to find
them at unexpected times.

1. Special Order

An organization or a business may order a special piece of cut glass to present to a
retiree or a winner of a contest, to mention a few. These include bowling pins or
possibly this chalice (P 1035). An individual may order an anniversary gift. Some of
the special order pieces have inscriptions on the glass, noting the event and the date.

2. Novelties

From time to time you will see one of a kind novelties. This plate obviously
commemorates the birth of the United States (L 1036). This loving cup illustrates
novelty in cut glass (L 1037). A silver stand for a flower pot (P 1038) and this car vase
(C 1039) suggest other novelties.

L 1037. A one-of-a-kind novelty in a loving cup,
12.5 by 8 inches.

P 1035. A 12-inch chalice in Russian Pattern,
probably bought on special order.

P 1038. A silver holder for a
flower pot, 10 by 6 inches,
ranks as a novelty.

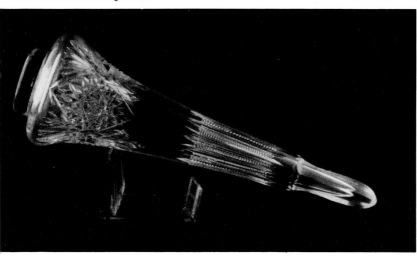

C 1039. A 10-inch, car vase comes under novelty.

C 1040. A whimsey in a 2-inch cologne.

3. Whimsies

At the end of the day the craftsmen could use the remaining molton metal to make small pieces called whimsies, such as this cologne (C 1040). A carafe and tumbler, called an eye opener, contains a Hawkes signature (C 1041).

4. Small Pieces

Keep your eyes open for small pieces with a quality rating. For the desk you may find a paperweight (C 1042) or a mucilage pot ((C 1043). Look for an interesting, small lamp (C 1044), a candleholder (C 1045), or an ash tray (P 1046).

Pieces for the dresser may include a mirror (C 1047) and a brush (C 1048) with a cut glass handle. The dresser may have room for a roseball (C 1049) or a violet vase (C 1050).

Perhaps a table setting offers the greatest variety of small pieces, such as a napkin ring (C 1051), a master salt (S 1052), a mustard pot (C 1053), or a catsup bottle (C 1054). If spirits appeal to you, consider a lady's flask (C 1055), a handled whiskey tumbler (C 1056), or a cherry bottle (C 1057).

Acquiring these small pieces add enjoyment to collecting. Yet collecting cut glass reaches beyond buying. You need to maintain the collection.

C 1043. A mucilage pot signed Clark.

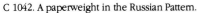

C 1041. A whimsey signed Hawkes in a bedroom set three inches tall.

C 1042. A paperweight in the Russian Pattern.

C 1044. A 6-inch oil lamp in strawberry diamond.

C 1045. A candleholder that adds to any collection.

P 1046. A 6-inch ash tray with holder for matches.

C 1047. A cut glass handle on a hand mirror.

C 1049. A 3-inch, tall roseball on three knobby feet.

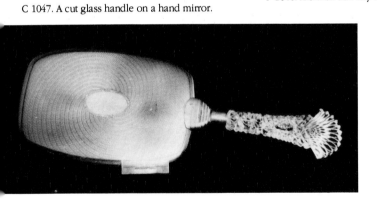

C 1048. A hairbrush with a cut glass handle.

C 1050. A 2.5-inch violet vase.

C 1051. A 1.5-inch napkin ring signed by Pitkin & Brooks.

C 1052. A 3-inch table salt.

C 1053. A mustard with a silver top in a unique shape.

C 1054. A catsup, 5.5 inches tall, in ornate pattern, decorated stopper, and honeycombed handle.

C 1055. A 4-inch, lady's flask.

C 1056. A whiskey tumbler with a handle.

C 1057. A 6-inch cherry bottle in Viceroy Pattern by Bergen.

Chapter 10

Maintaining a Collection

Cut glass requires no more care than any other fine antique. If you plan ahead, you can eliminate unnecessary work. Perhaps these tips will help you organize and maintain your collection.

DISPLAYING YOUR COLLECTION

Like most antiques cut glass requires displaying to enjoy it yourself and to share it with others. Keep your pieces in mind when you study the decor and available space in your home.

1. Placement of Individual Pieces

Study the rooms in your home and locate places where you may display individual pieces. The guest bedroom offers display space on a dresser. You may choose large ones, as a jewel, handkerchief, or glove box, for display. Use smaller pieces, such as cologne, puff box, hair receiver, or picture frame, to accent the larger ones. Place a lamp or night set on a bedside table.

The dining area provides places for exhibiting cut glass. A flower center or a bowl and candlesticks can grace the middle of the dining table. A buffet has space for a tall comport, decanter and wines set, or a small punch bowl.

In the living room a vase or a clock adds beauty to a mantle over a fireplace. A lamp or vase enhances any occasional table. A look around the room will reveal other spaces. Blend these individual pieces with the decor so they add a touch of elegance.

2. Cabinets

Check the available space for cabinets. If you don't already own a cabinet, you may want to buy one with glass doors as this protects the glass from breaking as well as needing frequent washing. You may prefer to buy an old one with rounded front and replace the wooden shelves with heavy glass ones. By all means add a light.

Look for spaces for corner cabinets with glass doors. These hold considerable glass but prove costly if antique. Do check in your area for a cabinet maker who can build a corner one to fit the space you have available and at less cost. After all, you want to show the glass and not so much the cabinet.

Modern breakfronts display glass very well. These offer adjustable shelves and the protection of glass doors. The adjustable shelves will accommodate tall or short pieces. The sectional divisions enables you to feature trays or wine sets. Sometimes you can find these breakfronts in good condition at a secondhand store or auction at a reasonable price.

Some collectors have built cabinets in a bare wall space, such as a hallway or beside a fireplace. The trouble with these, if you move, you can't take the cabinets with you. Some extensive collectors have added or converted house space into a glass room. They line the walls with cabinets, open or with glass doors.

No matter which type of cabinet you use to display your glass. do not choose a spot where strong sunlight may reach it or extremes of hot or cold atmosphere. Avoid places near windows, ventilators, or heating vents. The air in these areas produce a substance that dulls the sparkle of the glass and requires cleaning more often.

3. Arrangement in Cabinets

By all means take plenty of time to plan the arrangement of glass in a cabinet. Pieces, such as plates, trays or bonbons, look lovelier when you put them on holders that provide a full view. You have a wide choice of holders: clear, wire, metal, plastic, wooden, or plastic coated you can bend slightly. These last ones come in several sizes and give extra support to a piece in case of an earthquake. Shop for holders at craft stores, art supply shops, or antiques shows.

When you arrange pieces in a cabinet do place the heavier ones on the lower shelves. Pay particular attention to smaller but heavy pieces, such as a large knife rest, ink well, or weighted-base comports. If an earthquake or cyclone should force open the doors of a cabinet and push out pieces, these heavy items will not fall on top of those thrown from the lower shelves. Never stack a piece inside of another.

CLEANING YOUR GLASS

If you collect the tools you need to wash your glass before you begin, you will save much time.

1. Procedure

You will need two plastic tubs, a beach towel, a cotton or linen dish towel, and various cleaning brushes for washing the exterior. You have a choice of brushes for cleaning the exterior: soft bristle one, a doctor's plastic scrub brush, or a fingernail scrub brush with plastic bristles. None of these will scratch.

You will need a bottle brush for cleaning the inside of certain pieces. A bottle brush with a bent handle cleans inside of pieces with narrow necks and ball shapes, such as a decanter or carafe.

Choose a mild detergent. Never use ammonia. Some dealers and collectors prefer Crystal Wash (P. O. Box 394, Pasadena, CA 91031) as it gives an excellent sparkle and seems to place a protective coating on pieces.

Fill the plastic tubs with cold water and add the amount of Crystal Wash stated in the directions or enough detergent for a slight soapiness in one. Scrub the pieces with the brush and rinse in the second tub. Place on the beach towel atop a flat surface and let drain. When dry, rub with the cotton towel. With decanters, jugs, and such shapes, place a dish draining rack on the beach towel. Turn the pieces upside down and drain overnight. Do leave the stoppers out of decanters, colognes, and such for several days to give the inside time to dry thoroughly.

2. Helpful Hints

If you use Crystal Wash, you can peridically rub the pieces on the outside with a damp cloth and return the sparkle. Sometimes you need only dust the piece to restore the shine and can put off washing again. A manager of a modern crystal shop used rubbing alcohol in a mixture of two parts to one of water. She placed the fluid in a bottle and sprayed the pieces dulled from handling or the atmosphere. The alcohol evaporates quickly.

Other collectors contributed these hints. Sometimes a vase that held wired silk flowers or a bell with a wired clapper gets rust on the glass. Use Rust Off sparingly to remove the stain.

At times sediment forms in vases and decanters, and the bottle brush will not remove it. Fill the piece with Simple Green concentrate and leave overnight. Return the liquid to its container and rinse the piece with cold water. If not completely clear, then fill with Simple Green and leave overnight again. You may need to take a long-stem cotton swab and loosen the sediment. Naval Jelly will also remove sediment if placed in a piece overnight. If still not completely clear, you probably have a "sick" piece that needs a specialist to clean it.

How often you wash your cut glass depends on its exposure to atmosphere that dulls the sparkle. The less you wash your cut glass, the better. Any handling, especially of slippery, wet glass, increased the risk of damaging or breaking it. Never under any circumstances clean your cut glass in an automatic dish washer.

3. Glass Protection

If you live in an area where you get exposed frequently to cyclones or earthquakes, you may want to wire a cabinet to a wall stud. Use eye screws for the wall studs and the cabinet. Connect these with a strong wire, leaving enough slack for the cabinet to rock two inches back and forth or side to side. This gives extra earthquake protection.

You may want to anchor pieces inside the cabinet to prevent them from knocking against each other or falling over. You can buy Stickem or Crystal Saver at the hardware store or garden shop. A small bit under the base will hold the piece in one location, preventing bumping against another nearby, and it does not mar the furniture. By gently twisting the piece, you remove it if necessary. You may want to stick individual pieces near traffic areas for protection.

RECORD KEEPING

Everyone needs to keep records of pieces in a collection. As soon as you buy a piece, make a record while the facts remain fresh in your mind.

1. File Card

A 4 by 6-inch file card should contain this basic information.

Shape: give the catalog name such as jug.

Number: You may want to give the piece your own number or, if insured, that of the insurance company. Type the number at the side end of a self-stick, address label. Then cut off the number as narrowly as possible and place on a deep, under miter or any inconspicious place on the piece.

Description: give the dimensions, the miter outline, and the motifs.

Condition: note any chips, flakes and the like.

Signature: name the company or describe the unknown signature and give location of either. Otherwise add "none".

Pattern: name the pattern and the company and state source. If not identified, put "unknown."

Repairs: if you have the piece repaired, describe and give the cost.

Cost, Date, and Value: across the bottom of the card give the original cost, date of purchase and value. If undervalued, raise to current one.

New Evaluation: on the back of the card put original cost, present date, and new value. List the source of your increased value. Update about every three years.

The index card should look like this:

SHAPE	NUMBER
DESCRIPTION	
CONDITION	
SIGNATURE	
PATTERN	
REPAIRS AND COST	
ORIGNAL PRICE	DATE VALUE

Type this model on an index card and have duplicates printed or xeroxed. If you own a computer, print your own. You may want to attach your purchase slip to the card. If you can add a picture, all the better. Collectors find a picture of their piece in a printed source and make a copy to add to the card. Old catalogs have no copyright, so you can do a xerox of a piece. Most magazines do not copyright the issues, so you can make a copy of an illustration. In doing the copying, make sure you do not break the copyright law which permits you to duplicate for your personal use only.

If you have a talent for sketching, you can draw a picture similar to one in a patent record which shows the miter outline and one part of the completed pattern. If you have access to patent records and find your piece, you can lawfully xerox it. With a little thought you can think of other ways to get a picture of a piece and attach it to the file card.

2. Insurance

A number of insurance companies offer a fine arts policy that covers such things as damage from fire, breakage, earthquake, or theft—to name a few. The cost proves nominal as the company attaches this to your homeowners policy. Get in touch with your insurance agent for more information on the fine arts policy.

You will need to keep the policy up-to-date. When you buy a new piece, you add this to the insurance list. Most insurance companies require verification of value by an appraiser. Don't let this deter you. For the original list, a dealer who specializes in cut glass can do the verification from your file cards. As you add a piece, send in a copy of the sales slip signed by the dealer. When you no longer own a piece, delete it from the policy.

3. Upgrading

An important aspect of record keeping involves upgrading. Too many owners become sentimental about the glass they own and refuse to weed out the not so good pieces. Get a loose leaf notebook and study the pieces in your collection. Make a list of pieces you want to upgrade. Any time you see a piece with a better quality than the one you own—no matter how small—buy it. If you have a standard piece, you may want to replace it with a premium one. Keep this list current in your notebook.

You can always sell the old piece or trade it in as part payment for one you want. Possibly you can use it as a wedding gift to a young couple. The piece may match a set of another collector. Small pieces make excellent house gifts when you visit friends or when someone does you a big favor. Any time you see a quality piece of cut glass that seems underpriced, buy it!

4. Buy List

Always look ahead by making a list of pieces you want to buy. Random buying proves costly and sometimes a headache. Study your collection and list in your notebook the gaps you want to fill. As you read and study about cut glass, stay alert to some unusual pieces that would blend as well as round out your collection. Let dealers and other collectors know about your buy list.

Collectors often specialize in one shape, such as small plates, whiskey tumblers, or napkin rings. Others collect vases, carafes, and other larger pieces. When they upgrade, they sell excess pieces. Keep in touch with such collectors as you may find a piece on your buy list. Keep your buy list current. Finally, always buy what appeals to you and what you will enjoy owning.

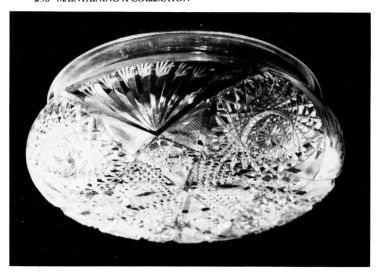

P 1058. A 9-inch dome for a ceiling light in Roman Pattern by Clark.

P 1059. A punch bowl, 13 by 10-inches with a pinwheel type of pattern.

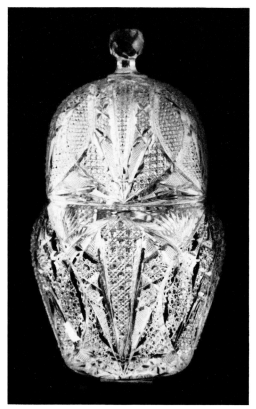

L 1060. A 10-inch jar with a dome top.

TODAY'S DREAM—TOMORROW'S REALITY

Every collector dreams of owning an exceptional piece of cut glass. Certain dealers do specialize in selling such pieces. Other dealers—collectors at heart—may keep such pieces for a time. So if you want to buy such a piece, alert dealers, collectors, and friends. These dream pieces will help you decide what you want.

1. Unique Pieces

This dome for a ceiling light Clark probably cut on special order in the Roman Pattern (P 1058). Imagine the elegant prisms it would flash around a room.

This heavy punch bowl has a scolloped foot, large fluted stem and border, and an ornate bowl (P 1059). Look for unusual punch bowls.

2. Pieces With Lids

Companies did not produce a large number of pieces with lids. Even then you want to look for an odd shape, heavily cut pattern, or a foot. A dome, similar to that for a butter or cheese dish, fits over the jar. The lid and jar match perfectly (L 1060).

This covered bonbon on a foot suggests another piece for your dream (P 1061). The piece has perfect balance in shape and pattern.

A massive bonbon with a most unusual lid and foot adds another plus with the Russian Pattern (P 1062). This piece, too, suggests special order.

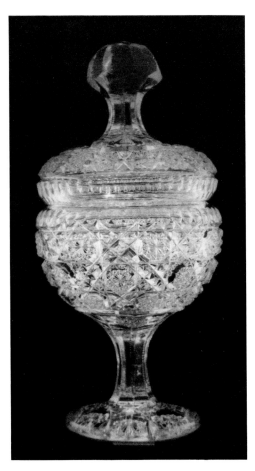

P 1061. A footed bonbon, 9 inches tall, with a matching lid.

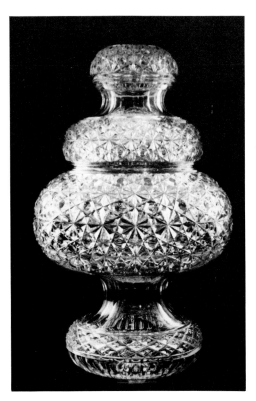

L 1062. A 14-inch bonbon with a cover in the Russian Pattern.

L 1063. A 30-inch tall vase in two parts.

L 1064. A footed rose globe, 11 by 7.5 inches, in Lorraine Pattern and signed Hawkes.

3. Flower Holders

Companies produced many flower holders but very few like these. This two-part vase combines the panel and miter and border outline. The minute cutting of the pattern leaves no blank space (L 1063).

Hawkes signed this footed rose globe in the Lorraine Pattern (L 1064). The scolloped base and cut knobby stem blend perfectly with the pattern.

This Hawkes vase in the Russian Pattern rates as a true treasure (L 1065). The scolloped base, balled step and heavy cutting make this piece most outstanding.

L 1065. A footed flower vase, 10 by 7.5 inches, in the Russian Pattern by Hawkes.

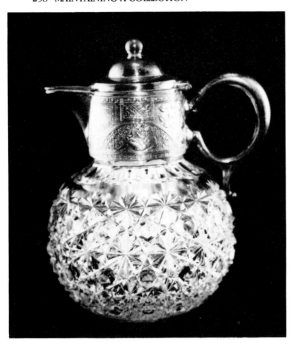

P 1066. An 8-inch jug in the Russian Pattern with silver top.

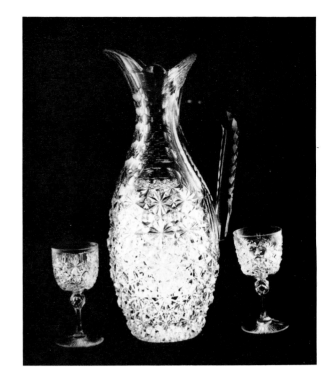

L 1067. A 12-inch champagne jug in Russian by Hawkes.

L 1068. A two-part salad or fruit bowl, 12-inches in diameter, in Persian Pattern by Hawkes.

4. Russian Pattern

Every collection needs a piece cut in the Russian Pattern. This pattern decorates one of a kind shape. The jug has a sterling silver fitting (P 1066). The lid extends to cover the spout, and handle has a thumb brace.

On very rare occasions you see a jug with two spouts. This jug has two spouts, decorated handle, and two matching wines—all in the Russian Pattern.

Finally, a fruit or salad bowl sits on a stand with four legs, cut in the Persian Pattern by Hawkes (L 1068). The piece has Shreve & Company on the silver.

Collecting brilliant cut glass has no limits. You think you have seen everything, and then another unique piece gets public acclaim. Consequently research never ends. More and more company records and old catalogs from estates expand the present knowledge. The continual search for authenticity adds fascination and challenge to collecting. In fact, you may make some discoveries on your own and do your part in preserving history.

One fact remains unchanged and unchallenged: American brilliant cut glass remains an irreplaceable part of our historical heritage. Always remember that once, for a period of forty years, the Americans produced the finest, brilliant cut glass in the world. So treasure you collection and enjoy its exquisite beauty.

Appendix

Signatures/Marks

C.G. ALFORD & COMPANY
New York, New York

BUFFALO CUT GLASS COMPANY
Batavia, New York

ALMY & THOMAS
Corning, New York

T.B. CLARK & COMPANY
Honesdale, Pennsylvania

AMERICAN WHOLESALE CORP.
Baltimore, Maryland

CORONA CUT GLASS COMPANY
Toledo, Ohio

M.J. AVERBECK MANUFACTURER
New York, New York

C. DORFLINGER & SONS
White Mills, Pennsylvania

J.D. BERGEN COMPANY
Meriden, Connecticut

O.F. EGGINTON COMPANY
Corning, New York

FRY

H.C. FRY GLASS COMPANY
Rochester, Pennsylvania

HOBBS, BROCKUNIER & COMPANY
Wheeling, West Virginia

HAWKES

T.G. HAWKES & COMPANY
Corning, New York

HOPE GLASS WORKS
Providence, Rhode Island

L. HINSBERGER CUT GLASS COMPANY
New York, New York

HUNT GLASS COMPANY
Corning, New York

HOARE

J. HOARE & COMPANY
Corning, New York

IORIO GLASS SHOP
Flemington, New Jersey

HOBBS GLASS COMPANY
Wheeling, West Virginia

IRVING CUT GLASS COMPANY
Honesdale, Pennsylvania

LAUREL CUT GLASS COMPANY
Jermyn, Pennsylvania

LYONS CUT GLASS COMPANY
Lyons, New York

LACKAWANNA CUT GLASS COMPANY
Scranton, Pennsylvania

MAJESTIC CUT GLASS COMPANY
Elmira, New York

LIBBEY GLASS COMPANY
Toledo, Ohio

MAPLE CITY GLASS COMPANY
Hawley, Pennsylvania

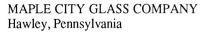

MC KANNA CUT GLASS COMPANY
Honesdale, Pennsylvania

LOWELL CUT GLASS COMPANY
Lowell, Massachusetts

C.F. M.C⁰

C. F. MONROE COMPANY
Meriden, Connecticut

NEWARK CUT GLASS COMPANY
Newark, New Jersey

PAIRPOINT CORPORATION
New Bedford, Massachusetts

F. X. PARSCHE & SON COMPANY
Chicago, Illinois

PITKIN & BROOKS
Chicago, Illinois

SENECA GLASS COMPANY
Morgantown, West Virginia

SIGNET GLASS COMPANY
Corning, New York

H. P. SINCLAIRE & COMPANY
Corning, New York

STERLING GLASS COMPANY
Cincinnati, Ohio

L. STRAUS & SONS
New York, New York

TAYLOR BROTHERS
Philadelphia, Pennsylvania

TUTHILL CUT GLASS COMPANY
Middletown, New York

VAN HEUSEN CHARLES COMPANY
Albany, New York

UNGER BROTHERS
Newark, New Jersey

WRIGHT RICH CUT GLASS COMPAN
Anderson, Indiana

CANADIAN CUT GLASS SIGNATURES

BIRKS

HAWKES
BIRKS

GUNDY, CLAPPERTON COMPANY
Toronto, Canada

HOUSE OF BIRKS
Montreal, Canada

RODEN BROTHERS, LTD.
Toronto, Canada

GOWANS, KENT & COMPANY LIMITED
Toronto, Canada

**NATIONAL ASSOCIATION OF
CUT GLASS MANUFACTURERS**

UNIDENTIFIED SIGNATURES

Bibliography

Avila, George C. *The Pairpoint Glass Story*. New Bedford, Mass.: Reynolds DeWalt Printing, Inc., 1968.
Boggess, Bill and Louise. *American Brilliant Cut Glass*. New York: Crown Publishers, Inc., 1977.
Boggess, Bill and Louise. *Identifying American Brilliant Cut Glass*. New York: Crown Publishers, Inc., 1984.
Boggess, Bill and Louise. *Identifying American Brilliant Cut Glass*. West Chester, Pennsylvania: Schiffer
        Publishing, Ltd., 1991. Revised and enlarged edition with value guide.
Collector's Illustrated Price Guide to Cut Glass. Paducah, Ky.: Collectors Books, 1977.
Daniel, Dorothy. *Cut and Engraved Glass 1771—1905*. New York: M. Barrows and Company, Inc., 1950.
-----. *Price Guide to American Cut Glass*. New York: William Morrow & Co., Inc., 1967.
DiBartolomeo, Robert E. *American Glass*. Princeton, N.J.: Pyne Press, 1974.
Ehrhardt, Alpha. *Cut Glass Price Guide*. Kansas City: Heart of America Press, 1973 (contains 8 catalogs).
Evers, Jo. *The Standard Cut Glass Value Guide*. Paducah, Ky.: Collectors Books, 1975 (contains 5 calalogs).
Farrar, Estelle Sinclaire. *H. P. Sinclaire, Jr. Glass Maker v. 1*. Garden City, N.Y.: Farrar Books, 1974 (contains
        inventory photographs).
----- and Jane Spillman. *The Complete Cut and Engraved Glass of Corning*. New York: Crown Publishers, Inc.,
        1979 (contains inventory pictures of Sinclaire glass).
Fauster, Carl U. *Libbey Glass*. Toledo, Ohio: Len Beach Press, 1979.
Feller, John Quentin. *Dorflinger America's Finest Glass, 1852-1921*. Marieta, Ohio: Antique Publications, 1988.
Fry Glass Club. *Encyclopedia of Fry Glass*. Paducah, Ky.: Collectors Books, 1989.
Gillander, William. *Treatise on Art of Glassmaking*. 1854. Second Edition.
Glass Container Manufacturers Institute. *Billions of Bottles*. New York, 1959.
Hodkin, F. W. and A. Cousen. *A Text Book of Glass Technology*. New York: D. Van Nostrand Company, 1925.
Hotchkiss, John F. *Cut Glass Handbook and Price Guide*. Des Moines, Iowa: Wallace-Homestead Book Co., 1970.
Kovel, Ralph M. and Terry H. *A Directory of American Silver, Pewter and Silver Plate*. New York: Crown
        Publishers, Inc., 1961.
Libbey Glass, 1818—1968. Toledo, Ohio: Toledo Museum of Art, 1968.
Lightner Museum. *American Brilliant Cut Glass, Masterpieces from Lightner Museum*. St. Augustine, Florida,
        1991.
McKearin, Helen and George S. *American Glass*. New York: Crown Publishers, Inc., 1946.
Mebane, John. *Collecting Bride Baskets*. Des Moines, Iowa: Wallace-Homestead Books Co., 1976.
Newman, Harold. *An Illustrated Dictionary of Glass*. London: Thames Publishing Company, 1977.
Oliver, Elizabeth. *American Antique Glass*. New York: Golden Press, 1977.
Padgett, Leonard. *Pairpoint Glass*. Des Moines, Iowa: Wallace-Homestead Book Co., 1979.
Pearson, J. Michael. *Encyclopedia of American Cut and Engraved Glass*. 3 volumes, Miami Beach, Florida,
        1975—1977.
----- and Dorothy T. *American Cut Glass For Discriminating Collector*. New York, 1965.
----- and Dorothy T. *American Cut Glass Collections*. Miami Beach, Florida, 1969.
Pennsylvania Glassware, 1870—1904. Princeton: The Pryne Press, 1972.
Phillips, David Brandon. *Objects of American Brilliant Period Cut and Engraved Glass, 1880—1910*. 1985.
Rainwater, Dorothy T. *Encyclopedia of American Silver Manufacturers*. West Chester, Pa.: Schiffer Publishing,
        Ltd., 1986.
Revi, Albert Christian. *American Cut and Engraved Glass*. New York: Thomas Nelson & Sons, 1965.
----- *The Spinning Wheel's Complete Book of Antiques*. New York: Grosset & Dunlap, 1972.
Schroeder, Bill. *Cut Glass*. Paducah, Ky.: Collectors Books, 1977.
Spillman, Jane Shadel. *Glass Tableware and Vases*. New York: Alfred A. Knopf, Inc., 1982.
Stevens, George. *Canadian Glass, 1825—1925*. Toronto: Ryerson Press, 1967.
Swan, Martha Louise. *American Cut and Engraved Glass of the Brilliant Period*. Lonbard, Ill.: Wallace-Homestead
        Book Company, 1986.
Victoria and Albert Museum. *Glass Table-Ware*. 1947.
Waher, Bettye W. *The Hawkes Hunter, 1880—1962*. 1984.
Warman, Edwin G. *American Cut Glass*. Uniontown, Pa.: E.G.Warman Publishing, Inc., 1954.
Weiner, Herbert and Freda Lipkowitz. *Rarities in American Cut Glass*. Houston: Collectors House of Books
        Publishing Co., 1975.
Wilson, Kenneth M. *Glass in New England*. Old Stourbridge Meriden Gravure Company. Meriden, Connecticut,
        1969.

Catalogs

Alford Cut Glass, 1904.
Ben Allen & Co., 1924.
Averheck Rich Cut Glass: catalog #104, undated.
Bergen Cut Glass Company: 1904-1905, 1907-1908, 2 undated.
Blackmer Cut Glass: 1904, 1906-1907.
Buffalo Cut Glass Company catalog.
T. B. Clark & Company: 1896, 1901, undated, 1905, 1908, undated.
Covington Cut Glass Company, 1915.
C. Dorflinger & Sons: catalog #51, 1881-1921, undated.
----- catalog Kalana Art Glass.
0. F . Egginton Company catalog.
Elmira Cut Glass Company catalog.
Empire Cut Glass Company: 1906, 1910, 1912.
H. C. Fry Glass Company catalog.
Gundy-Clapperton Company: 1909, 1915.
T. G. Hawkes & Company: American Cut Glass Association catalog, 14 catalogs of Brilliant Period, two late
        catalogs and advertising booklet, undated.
Higgins & Seiter: 1893, 1899, #7, #17, #19.
J. Hoare & Company: three catalogs with no dates, 1911 catalog, and undated scrapbook.
G. W. Huntley, 1913.
Irving Cut Glass Company, Inc. catalog.
Keystone Cut Glass Company catalog.
Kranz & Smith Company catalog.
Lackawanna Cut Glass Company; two catalogs.
Laurel Cut Glass Company: two catalogs; one 1907, other undated.
Libbey Glass Company: 1893, 1896, 1898, 1904, 1905, 1908, 1909, 1900-1910, c. 1920, 2 undated.
Liberty Cut Glass Works catalog
Linford Cut Glass Company catalog.
Lotus Cut Glass Company: No 49, No. 50.
Luzerne Cut Glass Company: two catalogs with no dates.
Maple City Glass Company: 1904 #3, 1906 #5, 1911 #10.
Marshall Field, 1896.
Meriden Cut Glass Company catalog.
C. F. Monroe Company catalog #6, other undated.
Mt. Washington Glass Works: 5 catalogs of Brilliant Period.
Niagara Cut Glass Company: two catalogs.
Ottawa Cut Glass Company, 1913.
Pairpoint Corporation: American Cut Glass Association catalog and 5 undated catalogs.
Parcel Post Cut Glass Company catalog.
F. X. Parsche & Sons Company catalog.
Phillips Cut Glass Company catalog.
Phoenix Glass Company: 1893 and one undated.
Pitkin & Brooks: 1907 and 3 undated.
Powelton Cut Glass Company catalog.
Quaker City Cut Glass Company: two catalogs undated.
Rochester Cut Glass Company catalog.
Roden Brothers, 1917.
Silver Plate and Sterling Silver catalogue of 1888 by W. G. Crook.
Sterling Cut Glass Company: two catalogs.
Steuben Glass Works catalog.
L. Straus & Sons, 1893.
Taylor Brothers: two catalogs.
F. B. Tinker, 2 undated catalogs.
Tuthill Cut Glass Company, The Connoisseur.
Unger Brothers: two catalogs: 1906 and one undated.
Unidentified Salesman's Catalogue, 1890—1905.
Unidentified catalog, possibly Hoare.
Val Saint-Lambert, 1908.
Wallenstein Mayer Company, 1913.
Waterford Glass Company, undated.
Wilcox Silver Plate Company, undated.

Index of Illustrated Patterns

Index of Colored Cut Glass Patterns

Index of Companies

Values Guide

We, the authors of this book, greatly emphasize that a value guide contains only a basic range of prices that requires adjustment to such factors as: geographical area, condition of the item, signature, rarity--to name only a few. Neither the authors nor the publisher assume any responsibility for any loss that occurs by using this value guide.

	Standard	Choice	Premium
BASKETS			
Bonbon	150-295	300-425	425-575
Flower 16"	600-850	1200-1500	1800-2200
BELL			
Small 4"-5"	125-175	175-275	275-450
Large 6"-7"	200-275	275-400	400-550
BONBON			
Handled 5"	60-100	100-175	200-275
Covered 6"	125-175	175-250	250-450
Footed 5"-6"	175-225	225-300	325-525
BOTTLES			
Bitters w/Top	150-200	200-275	275-300
Cologne 6"	275-350	375-475	500-950
Ketchup	100-175	250-325	325-475
Perfume 5"-6"	175-250	275-375	400-650
BOWLS			
Finger	75-100	150-300	325-450
Berry 8"	150-225	350-850	1000-3500
Low 10"	200-275	350-850	900-3500
Divided 9"	175-300	350-500	600-1200
Handled/Footed	175-300	350-500	600-1200
Orange 10"	175-225	250-400	450-1250
Whipped Cream 6"-7"	125-225	250-400	425-700
BOXES			
Glove	600-750	800-1400	1500-3500
Handkerchief	425-500	500-850	850-2000
Puff/Hair	75-125	150-250	275-450
Jewel (round)	475-600	600-900	900-2650
BUTTER			
Covered	300-475	500-750	750-1400
Pat	25-40	50-75	90-125
Tub	150-225	250-400	450-700
Stick/Fluff	100-175	225-400	550-900
CANDLESTICK			
Single 10"	150-225	250-325	350-600
Pair	375-550	900-1200	1400-2200
Candelabrum (single)	900-1200	1400-1750	1800-3700
CARAFES			
Regular	60-125	125-250	275-450
Night Cap	225-400	425-650	700-1000
CELERY			
Oval	75-175	200-325	350-600
Footed	n/a	950-1400	1450-2250
Upright	200-325	350-475	600-825
CHEESE			
Covered	175-275	325-600	650-1000
Cheese & Cracker	150-225	250-375	400-650
COMPOTES			
Squat	90-325	200-325	375-600
Tall 10"-12"	250-375	500-950	1000-2200
Covered	250-375	400-800	800-1700
Handled	175-250	275-575	750-1000
Divided	175-250	275-575	750-1000
DECANTERS			
Wine	350-900	1200-1500	1850-4250
Whiskey 12'	350-600	900-1600	1800-3800
Handled	475-900	1300-1800	1800-4000
Demijohn	650-975	1000-1500	1500-3500
Tantalus (2 bottle)	1000-1500	1500-2500	2500-4500
DISH			
Oval/Round 5"	75-175	200-425	450-1000
Square 8"-9"	450-850	900-1350	1400-2600
Covered dish	n/a	1250-2000	2000-3800
Handled	150-275	275-400	400-900
FLOWER HOLDER			
Center 10"	750-1000	1100-1600	1800-2800
Globe 7"	225-375	400-700	700-1400
Canoe 12"	550-800	800-1100	1200-1800
Ferner 8"	125-200	225-375	400-750
Violet	100-125	150-225	250-425
Footed Bowl	275-400	425-675	700-1000
Pot 6"	175-250	275-350	400-700
GLASSWARE			
Champagne	25-50	50-100	150-350
Claret	25-40	50-75	100-300
Wine	25-35	45-70	100-300
Cordial	20-30	40-60	70-100
Tumbler	20-30	50-100	100-350
Shot	20-35	45-70	85-400
Ale	40-80	90-150	150-350
Sherry	25-35	45-70	100-250
Mug	150-200	225-400	400-750
ICE			
Bowl	225-425	450-650	650-975
Tub	200-350	375-600	625-900
JARS			
Cracker	650-1000	1050-1600	1800-3600
Tobacco 7"	800-1200	1400-2400	2500-4000
Cigar 8"	850-1300	1500-2500	2600-4250
JUG			
Champagne	550-775	800-1400	1500-3200
Tankard	475-625	650-1250	1300-2200
Footed	500-675	700-1350	1400-2400
Lemonade	425-550	575-825	850-1400
Bulbous	625-775	800-1300	1400-2000
Silver Trim	725-900	1000-1600	1700-4800
LAMPS			
Oil 7"-8"	800-1100	1200-1800	1900-2600
Small	2000-3500	4000-6500	7000-12000
Tall	4500-6500	6500-9500	9500-27000
MISCELLANEOUS			
Loving Cup (small)	n/a	275-475	n/a
Loving Cup (large)	475-600	650-800	900-1200
Clock 5"-6"	400-500	525-650	675-900
Flask 4"	135-160	175-250	275-425
String Box	n/a	325-475	n/a
Muscilage	n/a	225-500	n/a
Paperweight	n/a	325-550	n/a
Toothpick	30-60	75-150	200-1500
NAPPIES			
No Handle 6"	50-80	80-150	200-700
One Handle 6"	60-85	100-175	225-750

Two Handle 7 "	85-125	150-225	275-900
Three Handle 5"-6"	125-165	200-275	325-950
OILS			
Small	125-175	190-275	300-575
Tall	150-190	200-375	400-775
Footed	225-300	350-850	900-2400
PICKLE/RELISH			
Scenic 8"	275-350	375-475	500-800
Handled	75-125	150-350	375-575
Oval	60-90	125-275	300-650
PLATES			
5"-6"	90-150	175-250	300-750
7"-8"	100-175	200-375	400-2200
9"-10"	200-275	300-400	400-2200
POTS			
Tea	1600-1800	1800-2500	2500-5500
Coffee	2500-3200	3200-5000	5000-8500
PUNCH BOWLS			
One Piece 14"	750-1500	1500-2200	2200-4500
Two Piece Tall 14"	1100-2000	2000-3500	3500-6000
Two Piece Squat 12"	1000-1500	1500-2500	2500-5000
Two Piece Small12"-14"	1000-1400	1400-2500	2500-5500
Two Piece Large15"-18"	1400-2200	2300-3800	3800-8000
SAUCERS			
Round 5"	60-90	100-225	225-800
Handled	60-90	100-225	225-800
SPOONER			
Upright	100-160	175-250	275-650
Footed	100-175	200-325	350-800
Tray	`90-150	175-250	250-550
SUGAR & CREAM			
Small	100-175	175-275	300-650
Medium	120-200	225-300	325-700
Large	200-275	300-475	500-1500
Footed	200-275	325-500	525-1500
Covered	175-25	275-475	500-1350
Lump Sugar	n/a	125-475	n/a
Sifter	n/a	250-475	n/a
SYRUP			
Small (all glass)	90-150	175-250	250-425
Small (silver top)	200-275	300-425	450-600
TRAYS			
Bread	`300-400	425-650	700-2400
Cake Low foot	375-625	650-775	800-2600
Cake Tall Footed	1800-2500	2500-5000	5000-8500
Two Piece			
Oval 10"-12"	500-800	850-1100	1200-3200
Oval 14"-18"	700-925	1000-1500	2200-4200
Rectangle 14"	600-800	900-1400	1500-4000
Round 12"-14"	600-800	850-1100	1200-3200
Handled 6"-8"	700-850	900-1200	1400-2800
Square 9"	450-850	900-1350	1400-2600
Acorn/Leaf	n/a	1400-1800	2000-4200
Shell	n/a	1500-2000	2000-5500
VASES			
Small 6"-8"	100-135	150-300	400-900
Medium 10"-14"	175-550	325-550	600-2000
Large 16"-20"	800-1300	1400-1800	2000-4200
Tubular 12"	175-300	350-600	800-2400
Urn	425-700	750-1050	1200-3800
Two Handled 12"	475-650	700-1100	1200-2600
Fan	400-475	500-750	800-1200
Hanging w/Chain	450-650	800-1200	1400-2800
Shower Five Piece	1600-1900	2000-2800	3000-3800
Epergne 25"-30"	4500-7500	7500-14000	15000-28000
Cornucopia	3200-3800	4000-5400	5500-7500